Global University for Sustainability Book Series

The book series aims to publish books and monographs drawing on the expertise of the Global U Founding Members by offering a succinct analysis of global crises affecting the ecological, social, political, and economic aspects, as well as to explore transformative visions and praxis for sustainability. Some books may be translated from their original language into English.

Lau Kin Chi · Huang Xiaomei · He Zhixiong

The Fukushima Catastrophe

To What End?

palgrave
macmillan

Lau Kin Chi
Lingnan University
Hong Kong, China

Huang Xiaomei
Hong Kong, China

He Zhixiong
Yongji, China

Translated by
Alice Chan
Lingnan University
Hong Kong, China

ISSN 2752-7379 ISSN 2752-7387 (electronic)
Global University for Sustainability Book Series
ISBN 978-981-99-1955-0 ISBN 978-981-99-1956-7 (eBook)
https://doi.org/10.1007/978-981-99-1956-7

Cover illustration: Alex Linch shutterstock.com

This Palgrave Macmillan imprint is published by the registered company Springer Nature Singapore Pte Ltd.
The registered company address is: 152 Beach Road, #21-01/04 Gateway East, Singapore 189721, Singapore

Paper in this product is recyclable.

About the Global U Book Series

Global University for Sustainability (Global U) is an international network of around 200 renowned scholars/activists, with a substantial number from Asia, Africa, and Latin America, apart from those from Europe and North America. They are academic scholars, peace activists, community workers, food producers, and rural reconstruction promoters, among others (please see https://our-global-u.org/ogu org/en/).

Since 2011, Global U has organized the South South Forum on Sustainability, with over 10 co-organizing universities and institutions from China and overseas. The Forum is a platform for dialogues and exchanges among grassroots and resistance practices in the production, dissemination, and use of knowledge as instruments of problematization and self-organization, as well as interactions among thinkers in search of paradigms for peace and justice. Since 2020, Global U has organized South South Dialogue on Sustainability Series, such as Venezuela in Struggles, Experiences with Indigenous Communities in Chiapas, African People's Struggles for Liberation, Constructing Alternative Paradigms in Brazil, and Rojava – Resistance, Resilience, and

Renewal. All proceedings of the Forums and Dialogues were video-recorded and uploaded to the Global U websites.

This book series aims to publish books and monographs drawing on the expertise of Global University Founding Members by offering a succinct analysis of global crises affecting the ecological, social, political, and economic aspects, as well as to explore transformative visions and praxis for sustainability.

The three main categories falling under this series are:

General analysis (e.g., history of political economy of a country; issue of sustainability, nuclear disasters, energy crisis, pandemic, climate change); with a focus on China and the global south.

Biographies, autobiographies, or anthologies of eminent thinkers from around the world, especially from Asia, Africa, and Latin America, connecting their personal trajectory to their thought and the larger context.

Analysis and interpretation of on-the-ground experiences highlighting how local communities negotiate with economic and other forces impacting on them and organize in alternative ways.

Lau Kin Chi
Sit Tsui

Foreword: Not Again, Please, Never Again

When asked to write a forward for this book, my mind immediately went back to what went through my head when a CNN journalist woke me up in London with news of the 11 March tsunami. They told me they had a photo of an explosion at the Fukushima Daiichi nuclear power plant and wanted to talk with me about what might be going on and what were the dangers. My first reaction—'Not again, please, never again'—was said out loud before I could switch into professional mode and ask what was known so far. I listened while my anguished thoughts flew to friends who lived along that North-Eastern Coast. Were they all right? Were they safe?

I had lived in Tokyo in the late 1970s, returning many times for meetings on abolishing nuclear weapons. I quickly checked email and some Japanese and international news services. Inevitably, the main focus was the horrific scenes and loss of lives in the fishing towns and villages along the coast. There was nothing about Fukushima in the Japanese news at first, but some concerns were being expressed in international media. The CNN interviewer asked me to discuss "if the reactors are exploding, what would be the worst that could happen?"

In the absence of reliable official information from Japanese sources, I described how the reactors were designed and spelled out the likely dangers if explosions cracked the reactor, for example, or the main core and spent fuel (stored in water above the reactor) lost their cooling baths of water and were exposed to air. This is what was actually happening. But necessary emergency responses were delayed as panicking bosses and officials tried to hide the appalling realities.

After my first interview, I received an email from a friend who was a nuclear expert with connections in both civil society and Japan's atomic energy establishment. Deeply worried about the inadequate official responses as the disaster at the Fukushima Daiichi nuclear plant unfolded, he sent updates and analyses to me and other international colleagues. His factual reports exposed the dangerous disinformation, reassurances and lies that were being promulgated by too many TEPCO and government spokespeople.

As wind and rain carried the devastating contamination into villages, hills, fields and seas, it became clear that no best-case scenario was possible. A humanitarian nightmare loomed. Key questions were how far would the contamination spread and how bad would it get. Our friend urged us to do whatever we could to highlight the serious dangers and get the facts out to the world's governments and media—to put pressure on TEPCO and the Japanese government to act more responsibly, and to properly inform and protect the Japanese people and environment.

Downwind of the Fukushima explosions, people who were hastily evacuated from homes that stood physically untouched by the tsunami's wall of water were anxious. But many later told me that they were mainly feeling sorry for the villagers whose seaside houses and schools had been turned into matchsticks. They never imagined that they themselves would never be able to return to their own precious homes. The quiet humanitarian catastrophe and long-term threats that were poisoning the air, fields and waterways across Fukushima province could scarcely be comprehended.

Over 15,000 untimely deaths of children, women and men occurred on that terrible day. The obvious destruction of lives and homes from the earthquake and tsunami was a cruel tragedy by any measure. Writing two weeks after Fukushima Daiichi was inundated, I noted, "We have to hope that the coolants and controls are fully restored, and that the severely damaged reactors at Fukushima and elsewhere will be made safe pending their dismantlement. It is a tragic lesson to see so much attention having to be spent on one dangerous facility when Japan needs to mobilize resources to provide for half a million survivors left homeless and traumatized".[1]

The story looked very different when I visited eighteen months after the deluge. Over 100,000 'radiation refugees' were 'still unable to return to their homes, schools, fields and factories'.[2] By 2012, it was inspiring to see how strongly communities of survivors were coming together to rebuild their shattered towns and villages along the northern coastline. The same could not be said about places downwind of the deadly radiation released when the nuclear reactors exploded. Fukushima's downwinders have been unable to rebuild their communities—their worst nightmares are still carrying on.

Downwinder Nightmares

I saw this for myself a year later, when I visited Fukushima in August 2012, together with doctors from several international countries. As one of three co-chairs of the recently formed International Campaign to Abolish Nuclear Weapons (ICAN), I had attended a major conference of the International Physicians for the Prevention of Nuclear War (IPPNW) in Hiroshima. ICAN's other co-chairs were Dr Tilman Ruff (the prime mover in founding ICAN in Australia) and Akira Kawasaki, an anti-nuclear campaigner who worked closely with the Peace Boat and *hibakusha* of Hiroshima and Nagasaki. Akira and a group of Japanese physicians (PANW) gave us briefings about the situation in Fukushima, and facilitated our travel to meet with activists and officials in Tokyo

---

[1] Rebecca Johnson, 'After Fukushima', *openDemocracy*, 24 March 2011 https://www.opendemocracy.net/en/5050/after-fukushima/

[2] Rebecca Johnson, 'Fukushima: a foreseeable consequence of nuclear dependency', *openDemocracy*, 16 March 2012, https://www.opendemocracy.net/en/5050/fukushima-foreseeable-consequence-of-nuclear-dependency/ See also the report by the Independent Investigative Commission on the Fukushima Daiichi Nuclear Accident, published by Yoichi Funabashi and Koichi Kitazawa, March 2012, https://ratical.org/radiation/Fukushima/IotFDNArpt.html

and Fukushima. They obtained permission for us to travel by bus from Fukushima City to the edge of the 'red zone'; beyond the red zone line, we were told, levels of contamination were too high to enter without gas masks and radiation suits.

The next few paragraphs are taken directly from my contemporaneous notes and photos from that August visit, some of which were published by openDemocracy in September 2012.[3]

> The fields, homes and roadside verges as the bus left Fukushima City were immaculately tidy, as expected in Japan. This was Japan's familiar rural landscape—pretty houses interspersed with fluorescent green rice paddies and dark green soya bean fields, with long greenhouse frames and poly-tunnels of tomatoes, peppers, cucumbers and other summer vegetables.
>
> A few miles out of the city the scene suddenly changed. Gone were the tidy squares of rice and other crops. Instead, a riot of wild vegetation climbed up buildings and telegraph poles, obscuring the welcoming road signs with their waving cartoon characters. Now the roads were practically empty of cars, though our bus passed a few police vehicles and heavy diggers.
>
> Like the boarded-up schools, some of the empty shops and houses still had gardens where bright flowers fought for space against the creeping weeds. In fields and lining the roadside we saw rows of bulging sacks. The local doctors on our bus explained that these were filled with contaminated topsoil and vegetation awaiting collection for disposal as radioactive waste.
>
> Decontamination is a never-ending job here, as rain washes more radiation down from the hills and forests into 'decontaminated' fields and gardens. Pink tape marked the boundary of a decontaminated area behind a health clinic we visited, but the doctors admitted this was relative. More radioactive substances washed down every time it rained. In front of the clinic, an electronic counter displayed current levels of radioactivity.
>
> For us, as temporary and middle-aged visitors, the radioactivity shouldn't be much of a problem, and we had knowledge and equipment to take basic precautions. But the radiation levels we encountered are not

[3] Rebecca Johnson, 'From Fukushima to Hinkley Point', *openDemocracy*, 18 September 2012 https://www.opendemocracy.net/en/5050/from-fukushima-to-hinkley-point/

healthy for babies or young children—or for parents with young children or women of child-bearing age.

The shocking implications of this became clear when we reached Kawauchi village. Around 16–21 km south-west of the crippled nuclear power station, Kawauchi is actually closer than the abandoned villages the bus had driven through earlier. That's because the wind at the time of the explosions and fires sent the main radiation plume toward the north-west, which suffered the heaviest levels of immediate contamination.

We met the local mayor, Yuko Endo, who expressed his determination to keep the village alive. He evaded questions about the nuclear power plant, but spoke of the evils of the evacuation, saying that 63 people from the area had died due to 'evacuation stress', and that the elderly suffered most as their communities were disrupted and they lost touch with their friends.

Kawauchi village spans the 20 km total exclusion zone, known locally as the 'red zone'. Rather than leave the area completely, some villagers chose to be evacuated from their homes inside the red zone to temporary housing that was built on the 'safer side' of the village. Such relocated villagers were primarily those who had worked at the power plant and were subsequently employed on various decontamination projects, some of which were much more dangerous than their previous jobs.

One woman dabbed at tears as she showed us round a tiny anonymous room in her evacuation hut. She spoke of her beloved home near the sea where she had lived with her son and his family. To protect his children, her son had moved to Tokyo and was now living with relatives. She stayed in response to the mayor's call to keep the community alive, but said that she misses her family deeply. Her final, sad question continues to haunt me: "How can we keep this village going without any children or young people?"

On the outskirts of Kawauchi, we stopped at a beautiful farmhouse near a little duck pond next to rice and soybean fields. Things looked almost normal. But the 67-year-old farmer, Sonoko Akimoto, told us that the ducks were being used as a means to monitor the levels of contamination.

She and her husband had practically retired and handed over to the next generation to run the family farm. But their children and grand-children had to be evacuated for their own safety after the nuclear power disaster. Now the elderly couple were alone and struggling to keep things going. She had tears in her eyes as she spoke of how she and her husband

> planted their crops this year in the knowledge that—like last year's—they would have to be dug up, bagged up and treated as radioactive waste. Maybe next year's crops could be eaten, she said hopefully, but her eyes looked forlornly into the distance. The clicking geiger counters warn of a bleaker future for these gentle farmers and their ducks and crops.
>
> In the fishing villages and towns that were flattened by the tsunami's heavy wall of water, there were thousands of immediate deaths. Eighteen months later these communities are ringing to the sounds of active rebuilding and the laughter of children. By contrast, the villages of Fukushima are quietly slipping into long-term depression and decline. Local doctors told me that as yet there are few signs of illness directly attributable to the outpourings of radioactivity. What worries them most are the raised levels of suicides and health problems due to the stress, evacuations and loss of livelihoods, families and lifetime friends and neighbors.

I used my writings to put the aftermath of the Fukushima nuclear disaster into a context of political and local relevance in my region. Against widespread public opposition, the UK's Conservative Government was pushing to sign contracts with France and China to build new nuclear power plants in Britain, including 'Hinkley C', a new type of reactor earmarked an aging nuclear complex on the Somerset Coast.

The 'Stop Hinkley Campaign' had made many contacts with citizens groups and Fukushima protesters in Japan. They sent me a leaflet with a map that depicted the evacuation zones if Hinkley were to suffer the kind of accident that caused fires and explosions at the Fukushima Daiichi nuclear power plant in March 2011. Hinkley lies on the Bristol Channel, a vulnerable tidal confluence between England and Wales that connects the Atlantic Ocean, 'English Channel' and Severn River system. The 'Stop Hinkley Campaign' map showed that "depending on wind direction for a radioactive plume, Cardiff [the Capital City of Wales], Taunton and Bristol are close enough to be turned into ghost towns bereft of children and women of child-bearing age".[4]

---

[4] Rebecca Johnson, 'From Fukushima to Hinkley Point', *openDemocracy*, 18 September 2012 https://www.opendemocracy.net/en/5050/from-fukushima-to-hinkley-point/

Never Again?

I applaud *The Fukushima Catastrophe—To What End?* and its authors and editors, Lau Kin Chi, Huang Xiaomei and He Zhixiong, because it analyzes how human and environmental risks are exacerbated by political and industrial policies that put profits above the protection of the people. Based on a variety of interviews with residents, farmers, nuclear officials, journalists and activists who have been affected by the Fukushima disaster, they underscore the personal, political and humanitarian impacts in testimonies, science and photos. Working closely with Japanese activists and journalists, their book and the important connections between civil-military nuclear developments and drivers, is relevant to the rest of the world as well as the people and policymakers of China and Japan.

It is important to learn the lessons from Fukushima. Far from justifying nuclear power, climate chaos makes the rush to nuclear even crazier. Sea level rises and increases in extreme weather will exacerbate nuclear risks. Power plants are built close to seas and rivers because of their insatiable need for cooling water. The nuclear industry is trying to revive itself at our expense, though it has still not solved the problems of decommissioning and radioactive waste disposal from fifty years of nuclear power operations.

The shock of the Russian invasion of Ukraine acts as an even more urgent warning—about the fundamental and existential risks attached to nuclear technologies used for nuclear weapons and for nuclear energy production. Nuclear weapons use atomic fission and fusion to threaten other countries and the whole world with extinction. Nuclear power production is an essential part of the nuclear weapons production cycle, while lying about providing 'cheap, safe, clean atoms for peace' and fossil-fuel-free energy for life.

Nuclear weapons can start a nuclear war not just by military intention, or as a result of human error, mistakes, miscalculations, or maybe nowadays by deliberate electronic hacking or spoofing attacks. By intention or mistake, if something goes seriously wrong with nuclear energy or weapons, the consequences are likely to be widespread, indiscriminate and out of all proportion to any energy or security benefits attached to these dangerous technologies in the first place.

Looking for Hope

The Fukushima Catastrophe—To What End? closes with a painting of Pandora opening 'her' box. I like how the authors of this book rethink that Greek myth. It chimed with the questions I had since first reading the story of 'Pandora's box' when I was a child. Most narratives portray Pandora as guilty of disobeying the gods' and unleashing all the evils of the world. Like these Chinese authors, I see Pandora differently.

Both the curious woman and the filled box of horrors were designed by Zeus and his patriarchal clique of greedy gods to punish Prometheus, another 'god', for sharing the gift of fire to bring warmth and light to humans who were cold and hungry. Zeus and his bully gods were furious because they wanted to keep Fire and its powers for themselves. Zeus persuaded his friends to join him in creating the box of horrors and this young girl. They imbued her with curiosity and many stereotypically attractive qualities and sent her to the brother of Prometheus as his bride. This was not a friendly gift—Pandora was designed to be the delivery vehicle for spreading multiple forms of evil, sickness and harm around the world. Yet, in the end, Pandora is not just a disobedient girl or manipulated delivery means; she stands as a courageous, caring young woman who questioned the orders she was supposed to obey. She makes me think of the many young people we can see at the forefront of movements for nuclear abolition, climate justice and peace. She stands alongside all the brave, passionate activists that enable humanity to hold onto Hope.

London, UK Rebecca Johnson

Rebecca Johnson is the Director and Founder of Acronym Institute for Disarmament Diplomacy as well as a co-founding strategist and organizer of the International Campaign to Abolish Nuclear Weapons (ICAN) that won the Nobel Peace Prize in 2017.

Foreword: Charting Contested Contours of Sustainability, Development, Social and Ecological Justice

After the 2011 Fukushima catastrophe, the production of nuclear energy had seen some restraints and rethinking, though contesting concerns about climate change have continued to energize support for it. Moreover, the Ukraine war has caused much political and economic churning around these issues, leading to a worryingly renewed push for the nuclear option. This book serves as a timely, critical reminder of the dangers of ignoring or obfuscating the multi-layered terrain of nuclear power, including its largely unaccounted for social and ecological costs, and the world's inability to deal with nuclear waste disposal.

This is also a timely project since global attention has now been drawn to the need for solidarity and collective responsibility to deal with the devastating environmental, economic and social consequences of the Covid-19 pandemic. Indeed fresh interdisciplinary perspectives are being sought to shape deeper understandings of terms such as 'sustainable' and 'development', even as countries in their own contexts are attempting to define and work toward the U.N. Sustainable Development Goals (SDGs) and Agenda 2030.

There had been major concerns about the European Commission proposing to give nuclear energy and natural gas a 'green' label under a new taxonomy of sustainable economic options, even before the Russian armed forces had invaded Ukraine. In July 2022 the European Parliament endorsed this decision, whereby nuclear power plants that could manage to safely dispose of radioactive waste would be deemed 'green', allowing them access to billions of euros in cheap loans and state subsidies. A heated debate on the terming of gas and nuclear power as 'sustainable' led critics beyond the fold of environmentalists to call it a form of institutional 'green-washing'. Ironically, even though Germany and France had opposing interests, Germany being pro-gas and France pro-nuclear, their joint backing of the endorsement manifested a mutual support to their energy and industrial policies.

It is significant to recall that after the Fukushima nuclear catastrophe in Japan, Germany had completely shifted away and decided to abolish nuclear power by 2022, committing to move to renewable energy sources. It has however remained heavily dependent on Russian gas, now an embroiled entity within the trade sanctions declared during the war. France meets 70 percent of its energy needs largely through aging nuclear reactors (half of the 56 reactors are closed for maintenance and repair), yet is estimated to have 25 percent reduced electricity production this year. Meanwhile it has prepared a blueprint budget of 51.7 billion euros to build around 14 next-generation reactors by 2035.

The questions that have agitated the nuclear debate during the Ukraine war are not only about energy options for other countries, but also about the imminent dangers of the fighting happening in the vicinity of its 15 nuclear reactors at four plants, that generate about half of its electricity. The Chernobyl nuclear power plant, in the process of being decommissioned, raised concerns reminiscent of the 1986 accident. Yet the European Nuclear Society and the American Nuclear Society dismissed any dangers at the plant sites, stating in a joint statement that "Nuclear power plants are not ominous facilities to be feared.... Rather, they have already played an invaluable role in reducing air pollution, cutting greenhouse gas emissions, and reducing dependence on fossil fuels. And their future potential is enormous".

(Steven Mufson and Claire Parker, April 15, 2022 Washington Post; https://www.washingtonpost.com/climate-environment/2022/04/15/nuclear-energy-europe-ukraine-war/). However, the Union of Concerned Scientists interrogated this stance declaring that the vulnerability of nuclear plants to the dangers of war should make people pause and seriously reconsider their deployment.

This book, therefore, comes at a significant juncture, with an urgent call for a propitious pause, ten years after one of the worst nuclear catastrophes at Fukushima, even as the world contends with the unprecedented Covid-19 pandemic. Beginning with a first-hand experience of the place and its people soon after the disaster, and the voices of the young reflecting on it today, the book adopts a critical humanistic approach. Accessing a wide range of sources dealing with technical, economic and sociopolitical dimensions, it engagingly addresses diverse issues that continue to haunt and persist, and calls for collective action.

It is indeed important for the young generation, which is expressing its fears and anger, while investing its agency to step in and re-frame its future. Greta Thunberg, the iconic young Swedish climate activist, unambiguously criticized the EU vote on nuclear power as sustainable, writing on Twitter: "This will delay a desperately needed real sustainable transition and deepen our dependency on Russian fuels. The hypocrisy is striking, but unfortunately not surprising".

The book brings into focus the urgent dilemmas and unasked questions about the contested contours of what constitutes 'sustainable' in the multiple and iniquitous trajectories of 'development'. Importantly, it does it from the vantage point of what is held as a highly technologically developed society. An analysis of the nuclear power industry in Japan helps serve as an elevated lighthouse, to shed light on the vast uncharted endangered ecology of human and non-human actors.

There are things we cannot afford to forget. Our collective intergenerational memory needs to be refreshed, to reappraise the ideas by which crises are invoked and public acceptance gets afforded to often irrevocable decisions. Japan, the first country where the atomic bomb was used to dismember its people, has had a complex history of cultural acceptance of nuclear energy. Ironically, its physicists had played an important role in claiming its right and duty to promote peaceful uses of the atom, while America had invoked 'atoms for peace' in the 50s; a subsequent oil crisis had lent strong support to the generation of nuclear power.

Taking the existing scholarship forward, this book makes a concerted effort and extends the circle of readership to engage with critical inter-disciplinary issues, by paying attention to different genres, the language, style and the visuals included. On the challenges of dealing with the public understanding of notions such as 'safe' or 'dangerous' radiation exposure, or about the problems of 'scienceplanation', it complements the discussions in an earlier book *'Lessons from Fukushima: Japanese Case Studies on Science, Technology and Society'* (Yuko Fujigaki (Ed.), Springer, 2015) and presents a substantively nuanced approach to the understanding of socio-techno-scientific issues with a focus on social and ecological justice.

New Delhi, India Anita Rampal

Anita Rampal is Professor and Dean (retired), Faculty of Education, University of Delhi, India. She is also Member, Executive Committee, All India People's Science Network.

Preface

Fukushima is a prefecture in northeast Japan, a mere 1.5 hours' drive from Tokyo. Fukushima is a large geographical area, with jurisdiction over 61 cities, towns and villages. Before the March 11, 2011, accident, the population was 2.3 million. It was notable in Japan for agriculture and mining, with products such as peaches, rice (e.g., the famous Koshihikari rice), pears, cherries, apples, Korean ginseng and so on. Many popular food items such as anglerfish and Aizu horse meat, as well as young people's favorite noodle dishes, the Kitakata Ramen and Shirakawa Ramen, all come from Fukushima.

On Chinese websites, there is very little information about Fukushima's history prior to 2011. The 2011 nuclear disaster is the watershed mark in Fukushima's history. 'Fukushima', literally meaning the Island of Happiness, has tragically come to be grounded in history with memories of the nuclear disaster, and the people of Fukushima, who should have been the author of the history of happiness, are forever handicapped.

Were there people who should be held accountable for the Fukushima accident? Yes. Were there negligence or blunders? Yes. Then, were those accountable people penalized? NO! Why?

There are too many 'whys' involved. Other than asking why, we should ask what lessons people have learnt from it and whether similar blunders will occur in the future. We should ask if the case of Fukushima became a catastrophe due to human error.

Twelve years have gone by. Other than in Japan, how many people still ask these questions? All over the world, news of the Covid-19 pandemic takes the headlines. People are probably most concerned about when it would be possible to go out, to travel and to discard the face masks. When Japan is mentioned, they would perhaps think that as the Olympic Games had indeed taken place in 2021, all must have been well. They might have no inkling that the people of Fukushima have already been displaced from their homes for over a decade.

Hong Kong, China — Lau Kin Chi
Hong Kong, China — Huang Xiaomei
Yongji, China — He Zhixiong

May 3, 2018, Iitate village. A mikoshi departed from the shrine where the big festival was held for the first time in ten years, traveled between the rapeseed planted for agricultural land preservation and the provisional temporary storage place of the contaminated soil. (Photo by Toyoda Naomi)

Futaba Town, December 21, 2015. Yuji Onuma and his wife resist the removal of the slogan advertising the nuclear power station behind them. When Mr. Onuma was in elementary school, the slogan "Nuclear energy represents our bright future" was raised in the area, and he believes that the slogan should be preserved as a negative example. (Photo by Toyoda Naomi)

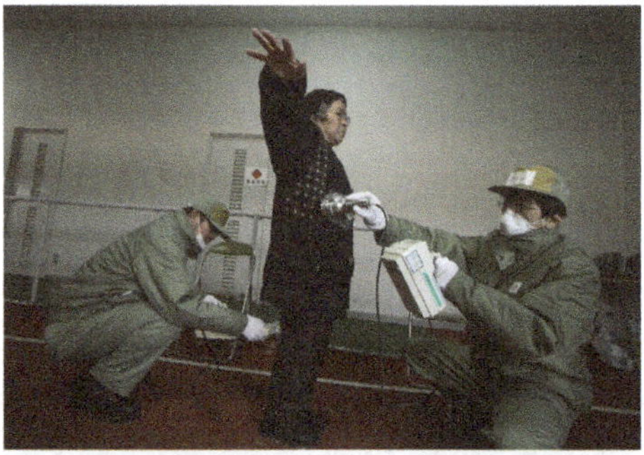

This lady who lived in the evacuation zone went to stay with relatives. She is being measured for radiation 'To reassure my grandchildren'. (Photo by Toyoda Naomi)

Futaba Town, March 11, 2016. Five years after the nuclear power plant explosion, the only people in the central area of Futaba were television crews and evacuees guiding them, wearing 'protective gear' that did not actually protect them from radiation. (Photo by Toyoda Naomi)

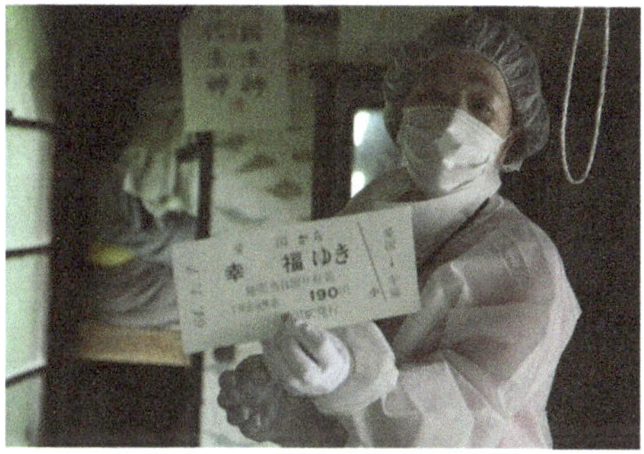

Namie Town, Tsushima, August 7, 2017. When they came home to sweep the ancestors' graves, they found the house destroyed by monkeys and wild boars. The ticket they recovered was a souvenir of their Hokkaido trip, and it says 'From Aikoku (patriot) Station to Kofuku (happiness) Station'. (Photo by Toyoda Naomi)

May 3, 2018, Iitate village. At the Big Festival, a row of about 120 people with mountain cars and shrine mikoshi paraded the inside zone of the village. There was a provisional temporary storage space for storing soil contaminated with radioactivity spread. (Photo by Toyoda Naomi)

Iitate Village, February 26, 2015. In a barn with no smell of hay or milk, a tablet inscription praying for the dead cattle declares that the accident at the nuclear power station was in fact a man-made disaster. (Photo by Toyoda Naomi)

Iitate Village, February 26, 2015. A morning meeting where workers are exposed to the radiation of black plastic bags containing nuclear-contaminated soil. More cleaners than evacuees have been recruited from across the country to do what is known as 'decontamination', including weeding, cleaning, mopping roofs and walls, and removing topsoil from fields. (Photo by Toyoda Naomi)

Iitate Village, September 18, 2017. Former dairy farmer Kenji Tanigawa is looking at the buckwheat flowers, which he was worried would be blown over by the typhoon. He said, "I don't think the buckwheat flowers produced in Iitate Village will sell". Last year, the radiation level was 26bq/kg, not zero. (Photo by Toyoda Naomi)

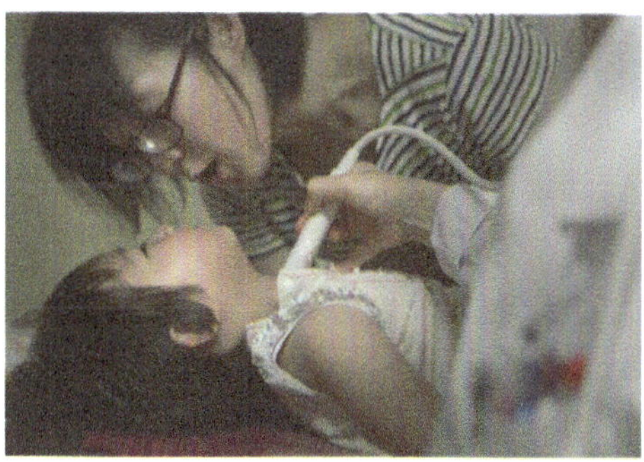

Koriyama City, June 18, 2016. As of January 2018, 194 children have been found to have thyroid cancer, and epidemiologists say the prevalence is 20 to 50 times higher than usual. However, the Fukushima prefectural government reiterates the official story: "It is unlikely to have been caused by the nuclear power plant accident". This statement did not ease the mothers' anxiety. (Photo by Toyoda Naomi)

Contents

About the Authors

Lau Kin Chi is Coordinator of Programme on Cultures of Sustainability at the Centre for Cultural Research and Development, Lingnan University, Hong Kong, China.

Huang Xiaomei is freelance translator and simultaneous interpreter based in Hong Kong, China.

He Zhixiong is Director of the Digital Section, Green Ground Rural Reconstruction Social Enterprise Alliance, China.

1

Introduction: No Solutions in Sight, Making Possible the Impossible—Lau Kin Chi

12 October 2012. It was a bright autumn day, with white clouds and a blue sky atop the poetic pastoral scene. I wound down the car window, wanting to take some photographs of the scenic countryside. My Japanese friends in the car, forgoing their usual good manners, exclaimed "Professor Lau Kin Chi, please shut the window right away!" Screaming at the same time was the radiometer that each of us was holding. Within seconds, the radiation level inside the car had risen sharply by many times.

It was exceptionally quiet outside. Those inside the car were nervous. Three of us were visitors to Japan, coming from China, India, and Thailand. The three guides were our Japanese friends, Professor Ohashi Masaaki, Ms. Fujioka Emiko and Mr. Takeuchi Toshiyuki. We came to Fukushima to visit the villagers in several sites. Entry was permitted during the day but at night this area was still cordoned off. One home we visited was that of a farmer, Mr. Nemoto Koichi, in Odakaku, Minami-soma. Inside his home, Mr. Koichi and his wife served us hot tea and

K. C. Lau et al., *The Fukushima Catastrophe*, Global University for Sustainability Book Series, https://doi.org/10.1007/978-981-99-1956-7_1

apples, while telling us how they would drive for an hour every day to come back to their home here from the temporary accommodation in town, to cultivate the produce that would not and could not be sold. How else would they while away the time if not going to the fields? They spoke calmly, no hint of anger or regret. We deliberately drank our tea slowly so that the hosts would not be serving more, and occasionally forced down a slice of apple. We were aware that the water for making tea came from the well there, and the apples were picked from the tree in the backyard.

Left to right: Fujioka Emiko, Mrs. and Mr. Nemoto Koichi (Photo by Lau Kin Chi)

Our group then went to the village Iitate to visit the home of a dairy farmer. The car arrived in front of a stylish house and stopped. We were told to be back inside the car within two minutes.

The house of Hasegawa Kenji, to which he could not return (Photo by Lau Kin Chi)

The abandoned milk factory of Hasegawa Kenji (Photo by Lau Kin Chi)

The people were gone, so were the cows. All that remained was emptiness. We measured the radiation level around the flower plot in front of the house. It was 3.35 micro-sieverts per hour, way over the standard safety limit of 0.23 micro-sieverts per hour stipulated by the government.

We hurried back to the car and drove to a temporary resettlement site to meet the house's owners, Mr. Hasegawa Kenji and his wife.

They talked about the earthquake, the tsunami, the explosion of the nuclear power plant and the evacuation. They showed us the government's decontamination plan—the outside walls of the house would be jet-sprayed with water. With that, they were supposed to be able to move back. However, the government would not take responsibility for cleaning the contaminated material that had been washed off the house into the fields, and the residents were advised not to stay outdoors or to farm in the fields. The villagers were divided in their thinking—Mr. Hasegawa Kenji and his wife felt that they would not be able to go back to live in the village, and hoped the government would relocate the entire village, at any rate keep them together. The village chief, however, was inclined to await moving back in due course.

Mr. and Mrs. Hasegawa in the shared office in the temporary resettlement site (Photo by Lau Kin Chi)

Mr. Hasegawa Kenji showed us pictures to explain what happened. What had overwhelmed me the most was the story of another dairy farmer, Mr. Sugano Shigekiyo. After the nuclear disaster, he had to send all his dairy cows to the slaughterhouse. After sending them off, he tearfully set up a commemoration-tablet for the cows in the empty shed, wrote his last words requesting his sister to pay off personal debts such as to the carpenter, then committed suicide.

Image shown by Hasegawa Kenji of Sugano Shigekiyo sending the herd to the slaughterhouse

The empty shed, with the commemoration tablet for the deceased cattle standing alone (Photo by Toyoda Naomi)

I could not put away from my mind the scene of the dairy farmer commemorating the spirits of the cows then following them into oblivion. Those to atone for the cows should not have been the dairy farmer.

The last words of the farmer that committed suicide: "My gratitude to sister who cared for me all the time. I have experienced my 2011(June 10, 1.30 pm). I am so sorry, please pay back the carpenter with my insurance money. If there had not been a nuclear accident… Do not be defeated by the nuclear accident, please go on with the management of the farm. It is unfortunate to be walking in front. I have no more strength to go on" (Photo provided by Hasegawa Kenji)

The visit to Fukushima could only last for one day. Our Japanese friends were worried about exposing us to the colorless and odorless radiation. Their continuous concern and cautions had the effect of scaring us further. However, the farewell dinner at Fukushima City had enlightened me with a glimpse of pure beauty and hope.

Left to right: Lau Kin Chi (China), Ohashi Masaaki (Japan), Hasegawa Kenji (Japan), Vinod Raina (India), Supara Janchitfah (Thailand)

I was chatting with Fujioka Emiko. She said she lived in Tokyo originally and her husband had a very good job with a foundation. They had a good life. After 3.11, she joined some voluntary support activities. Having come in touch with the locals, the women, the young and the elderly, she had a strong desire to help them rebuild their homes and did not want to return to Tokyo. Yet her husband did not want to come with her. They divorced. I asked her, "Even in Fukushima City the radiation level is above safety level, let alone in villages within the disaster zone. Going there regularly, are you not worried about radiation exposure?" She said calmly, "I am already forty. I am not worried about radiation. I simply want the generation of children to live a good life." Her words were spoken with simplicity and modesty, no sense of heroic resolve, no sacrificial sentiment. She was in the prime of her life yet had looked death calmly in the face. And she was not doing it for her own family. She was extending her love to the children and elderlies of other families. She was an ordinary person, yet so extraordinary.

Left to right: Ohashi Masaaki, Vinod Raina, Fujioka Emiko; first on the right: Takeuchi Toshiyuki (Photo by Lau Kin Chi)

That day, under the bright sunlight I had seen the invisible presence of the radiation hazard, yet in an ordinary person I just came to be acquainted I had seen unflinching courage. So what if there are no solutions yet? Should we do no more than being angry and afraid at the injuries and deaths brought on by the blunders of others? What I saw was the refusal to live a perfunctory life. The tragedy had called up the people's indomitable courage, initiated the sublimation of their vitality and creativity. So what if one is to bear the pain? So what if one is to face death? To follow one's heart and die for a cause is well worth it.

With those mixed feelings welling up in me, I combed through my materials in English and Chinese, and compiled two collections of essays for private circulation among friends and students. Later, it occurred to me that I should produce a book to have more people caring, thinking, and taking action over what happened in Fukushima. In this endeavor I have been greatly supported by friends in China and Japan, and would like to give special thanks to Sun Ge, Wang Xuan, Dai Jinhua, Wen Tiejin, Ye Tong, Teng Wei, Zhao Ling, Lam Tsz Man, Wang Ping, Muto

Ichiyo, Ohashi Masaaki, Fujioka Emiko, Takeuchi Toshiyuki, Aihara Keiko, Ikegami Yoshihiro, Ando Nakao.... I am also deeply grateful to my two co-authors Huang Xiaomei and He Zhixiong, the translator Alice Chan, as well as the Global University for Sustainability team that has worked with me over these many years. Last but not least, my gratitude to the many volunteers who have dedicated their time and resource on our common cause.

[This is introduction to the Chinese simplified character edition of the book published by Joint Publishers]

2

Introduction: Education for Ecological Justice and Social Justice—Cultivating the Capacity for Affect, Thinking, Autonomy and Action—Lau Kin Chi

In May 2021, *Fukushima, Island of Fortune or Contamination: Interrogation after Ten Years* (《福岛/辐岛：十年回首诘问》, in Simplified Chinese) was published by Beijing Joint Publishers. Then in February 2022, the traditional Chinese character version of this book was published by Cosmos Books in Hong Kong, entitled《福岛/辐岛：喁点是福是祸?》. Facing the insolvable catastrophe, all we can do is make the cry: "Knowing that it is not possible, we still need to make it possible!"

I would like to take opportunity of the Fukushima tragedy's profound lessons to discuss some of my experiences during the course of my 30-year teaching in cultivating values for ecological justice and soci0-economic justice among students.

In the spring and summer of 2021, news from Japan caught the mainstream media worldwide. On one side, the Japanese government has threatened to discharge the Fukushima nuclear wastewater into the ocean, raising protests both at home and abroad; on the other side, with the Covid-19 pandemic still around, the Olympic gold medal list was tracked day and night. The tone of the news, with indignation on one

K. C. Lau et al., *The Fukushima Catastrophe*, Global University for Sustainability Book Series, https://doi.org/10.1007/978-981-99-1956-7_2

side and excitement on the other, had both to do with the Fukushima nuclear disaster.

The Tokyo Olympics

After the Fukushima nuclear accident on March 11, 2011, the Japanese government should have been putting every effort onto relief and cleaning up. However, just four months after, the Japanese Olympic Committee selected Tokyo as the host city to bid for the 2020 Olympic Games. Having succeeded in the bid in 2013, the Japanese government invested an enormous amount of money and resources into construction of the Olympic games venues, resulting in price hikes of building material and shortage of labor in the disaster region. The Tokyo 2020 Olympic Games was named the "Olympics of Reconstruction" with the theme being "Fukushima Recovery", and the Olympic torch was named the "Flame of Recovery". The J-Village Sports Complex in Fukushima would be the first stop for the Olympic torch relay on March 25, 2021. The J-Village is located only 20 kilometers from the nuclear power plant. It was converted into a disaster relief center after the March 11, 2011 catastrophe. Thousands of workers were dispatched from here every day to work at the Daiichi nuclear power plant. This image, a reminder that the Fukushima disaster is still being dealt with, is to be completely turned around, from workers wearing radiation protection gear and gas masks to athletes carrying the Olympic flame with valiant vigor.

At the opening ceremony of the Tokyo Olympics, in the empty arena without any audience, the song 'Imagine' was played, that classic anti-war, pro-peace song by John Lennon of the Beatles. Yet what a con it was that tried to fool the public into thinking that "reconstruction" and "recovery" were already on the horizon!

The Tokyo Organizing Committee announced that the concept for the opening and closing ceremonies of the Olympic Games was "Moving Forward". Further, the theme for the opening ceremony was "United in Emotion" and that for the closing ceremony was "Worlds We Share". However, the rhetorically sculptured beautiful new world could not stop the public's discontent in reality: the pandemic and the debts.

The Tokyo Olympics was "united in emotion" with Covid-19. From January 3, 2020 to October 14, 2021, Japan, with a population of 125.8 million, had 1,712,649 confirmed cases of Covid-19 and 18,020 deaths.[1]

The Tokyo Olympics was "united in emotion" with debts. The official figure for the Tokyo Olympics spending was US$15.4 billion. That amount could build 300 hospitals in Japan with 300 beds each, or 1,200 elementary schools. An Oxford University study stated that it was the most expensive Olympics in history. The Japanese government auditors said that the actual spending could be twice as high.[2]

This "price" paid for the Olympics brought an important impact: to positively promote the "recovery" of Fukushima and divert the spotlight away from the unmanageable mess left behind by the nuclear disaster.

Radioactive Nuclear Contaminated Water

The Japanese government repeatedly spread the words in 2002 to test the waters, and then on April 13, 2021, it officially resolved to discharge more than 1 million tonnes of "diluted" nuclear wastewater into the ocean two years later, in order to free up storage tanks for the more heavily contaminated nuclear wastewater. Waves of criticism and protest from Japan, neighboring countries, as well as the Chinese and foreign media came up one after another. The "discharge of nuclear wastewater" has become the focus of public opinion, yet rarely does anyone ask the more fundamental question: Why is the storage facility always insufficient, and where does the 140 tonnes of nuclear wastewater come from every day? Not only do we have to ask about the disposal of the nuclear wastewater, but we must also ask: can the production of nuclear wastewater be stopped? The chapter "Heart of Darkness—The Molten Core" in this book has details on the desperate situation. Here I would merely point out a fact: after the 257 tons of nuclear fuel melted down in the core, the molten fuel rods became blended with other metallic material from the pressure vessel, and the total weight came to 880 tons. However, the projected dates for "initiating the cleanup" of Fukushima Daiichi reactors have been pushed back again and again, most recently to 2024–2028. That is, it would be 13 to 17 years after the incident that clean up would be "initiated".

This would have been a most simple question, yet why is the mainstream media rarely seen picking it up? The issue of nuclear wastewater could have led us to question and investigate the root problem, yet why does it have the opposite effect of diverting attention from the latter? The public should not blame the authorities entirely for misleading and deceiving them, but need to ask: all along, how our education, be it formal or inculcation through various cultural and media channels, been shaping our way of thinking and perception.

Personal Experience

Many Chinese have a blanket dislike of Japanese people, yet I have seen in many of my Japanese friends the noble temperament of facing up to the harsh reality and taking responsibility. Professor Muto Ichiyo, whom I deeply respect, was expelled from the University of Tokyo in 1950 where he was an undergraduate student, for moderating a campus anti-war rally. In the appendix of this book, "Buildup of Nuclear Armament Capability and the Post-War Statehood of Japan," Muto Ichiyo points out that the introduction of nuclear reactors into Japan in the 1950s was for the precise purpose of nuclear weapon capability ownership. Muto Ichiyo has never wavered from the course of opposing Japanese militarism.

Muto Ichiyo (right) giving a lecture in Hong Kong in 2014 (Photo with Lau Kin Chi [left])

Professor Ohashi Masaaki of Keisen Women's University, who arranged my visit to Fukushima a year and a half after the disaster, and who is also the director of the Japanese NGO Center for International Cooperation, on the day following the disaster had immediately organized the civilian rescue team to personally deliver relief supplies to families who remained in their homes within a 20 to 30 kilometer radius of the nuclear power plant. At the time, international rescue organizations had forbidden their staff from approaching the area because the radiation level there was too high.

In order to identify one another, Ohashi Masaaki wrote his name Ohashi and and his organization JANIC on his protective clothing

Ohashi Masaaki introduced me to Mr. Toyoda Naomi, an international photojournalist. Mr. Toyoda has been travelling to and from Fukushima continuously for ten years. Mr. Toyoda observed, "Ever since the day of the nuclear power plant explosion in March 2011, I have been covering and photographing Fukushima. In the ten days before that, I was photographing Ukraine and Belarus, 25 years after the Chernobyl accident to clean up. In Japan, companies that had, before the accident, propelled the construction of the nuclear power plant, surfaced in the radiation contaminated area after the accident, profiting from the massive taxes being paid by citizens. The project has used the name "reconstruction". The construction company's heavy machinery and large dump trucks entered towns and villages that were left uninhabited by the radiation disaster, initially to "decontaminate" the buildings and fields, after which the "decontaminated" houses, warehouses, factories, schools, etc. were successively demolished. (Can you understand this kind of contradiction?) The 10 years of Fukushima saw the wiping out of the original scene and the emergence of previously non-existent 'reconstructed buildings and reconstructed public relations centers'. Most of those people displaced and scattered by radioactivity will not be coming back. They will not come back in the next 200 or 300 years, before the radiation released from the nuclear power plant fades away. Certainly, there are a few who will be back with the feeling of their inseparability from the land, prepared to be exposed to radiation. I value this way of life of theirs. Through this way of life, they seem to be querying the world on the meaning of nuclear accidents and nuclear damage. I still travel to Fukushima, hoping to capture in my photographs the scene that will be erased and the human dignity that will be indelible."

Toyoda Naomi at his photo exhibition

Ms. Aihara Hiroko, a reporter for *Japan Perspective News*, has been following the situation of those residents who were evacuated and who have returned to their hometowns. She said, "Ten years have passed but a large number of people are still affected. More than 40,000 people are still refugees, separated far from their homes. There is a Japanese saying, 'Ten years is one era,' meaning ten years make one historical milestone, but I have serious doubts about the applicability of this saying to the Fukushima nuclear accident. 'Can we give this tragic accident a time limit?' My answer is 'absolutely not', because the nuclear accident and radiation disaster are still on-going, and we still heavily require the social support of the international nuclear abolition movement."

Mr. Abe Yashuhiro who runs a movie theater in Fukushima City, in an interview by Kiroho Aihara, had said, "When the nuclear accident happened, Fukushima was lonely amidst the difficult situation. Now, with COVID-19, the operation of movie theatre is even more difficult than during the doldrum of the nuclear accident. Yet mentally speaking, the feeling of loneliness is less because the whole world can experience the same feelings of isolation arising from COVID-19, hence the resonance of solidarity." Yes, in the anti-nuclear movement, there is a need for being "united in emotion". Aihara Hiroko has called on everyone to believe in the "miracle of humanity", to walk on the road of history together, to collect the fragmented pieces of the Stone of Hope and hold them in their palms. She is convinced that these fragments will be like the Big Dipper and the Southern Cross, shining and sparkling.

Japanese civil society representatives at the 6th South-South Forum on "Ecology, Technology and Community Politics", Hong Kong, Lingnan University, June 28, 2019, with Aihara Hiroko, *Japan Perspective News* (front row, third from right), Fujioka Emiko, Global Citizen Network Center, Fukushima, Japan (front row, second from right), Rebecca Johnson, Founding Chair of International Campaign to Abolish Nuclear Weapons (2017 Nobel Peace Prize winner) (front row, fourth from right), Lau Kin Chi (front row, fifth from right)

Ms. Fujioka Emiko, director of the Fukushima Global Citizenship Network, whom I met during my visit to Fukushima in October 2012, had left her comfortable home in Tokyo to serve the victims in Fukushima. I asked her at the time, "Aren't you afraid of radiation?" She said calmly, "I am already 40 years old." When I received the news in

May 2021 that she had cancer, I was very upset. She was unable to attend the online 8th South-South Forum on Sustainability due to her illness, and had urged us to send her the video of the Fukushima discussions.[3]

I prayed silently for Fujioka Emiko and for the victims of the nuclear disaster whose lives had been ruined.

Moving on Under Stress

These Japanese friends whom I deeply respect have taught me both rational and emotional awareness. In the classroom of the university, I have included ecological justice and social justice in the curriculum and explore with the students on themes such as nuclear power and weapons, financial capitalism, developmentalism, climate collapse, ecological crisis and so on. On September 19, 2011, Professor Sit Tsui of Southwest University and I joined the civil society anti-nuclear march in Tokyo in which 60,000 people participated. In 2016, the World Social Forum held a special session in Japan on the abolition of nuclear weapons/nuclear power. I arranged for Professor Sit Tsui and Miss Auyeung Lai Seung to bring three students from the Department of Cultural Studies at Lingnan University, Lee Chi Ying, Siu Wan Tong and Yeung Ching Kiu, to attend. In my article "Reflections on Modern Education and Violence from the Perspective of Ecological Justice", I cited the emotional and rational impact on them arising from this field trip as a case study.[4]

They visited Tomioka Town in Futaba County, less than 15 kilometers from the Fukushima Daiichi nuclear power plant. With limited resources, the Forum could only give each person a raincoat and a mask, and they could stay for only 15 minutes each time they got off the bus. Auyeung Lai Seung is angry: "The dilapidated houses were empty. It was like entering into a dimension of stillness, everything remained at that moment on March 11, 2011, when the tsunami engulfed them. It was also like entering an alien dimension—a ghost world. The nuclear disaster arising from the tsunami destroyed the quiet and simple life of the residents, and further, the radiation pollution of the environment has destroyed the homes of several generations. One year of nuclear power, ten thousand years of nuclear waste!"

On March 23–28, 2016, Sit Tsui (right) and Au Yeung Lai Seung (left) from Hong Kong took three Lingnan University Cultural Studies students to the Fukushima exclusion zone to study the situation of de-contamination workers oppressed by out-sourcing

After returning to Hong Kong, the three students wrote down their reflections. Yeung Ching Kiu said that she had shared the experience with her friends, yet they seemed to maintain the attitude of "minding their own business" and had no motivation to pay attention to the issue. All they would think about was to not go to Fukushima when they travel to Japan. Lee Chi Ying said, "It was because I had seen with my own eyes the de-contamination worker working in the fields with zero protective equipment, the piles and piles of nuclear contaminated material dumped at the foot of the beautiful hills, forests and fields, the readings on the radiation measurement instrument in my own hands, moreover because I had visited civil society organizations and witnessed their years of dedication, saw the embarrassment and silence of Fukushima residents when asked about the March 11 incident, …… it was all of these that constitute the real reason why I could be so confident when telling my friends about the current predicament in Fukushima after I came back. It was not only charts and figures I saw in speeches. One should not forget the lives that are behind the cold, detached words. Only the real-life stories and experiences could form the solid core of faith."

I was touched by the genuineness of the students.

Message to Teachers, Students, and Youths

Over the years, I have attempted to sort out with my students the violent history of modernism and "supremacy of science", that articulated into all forms of social injustice and ecological injustice. We refuse to see the world from the perspective of mainstream elites, instead have consciously concerned ourselves with the survival conditions of marginalized communities, listening to their cultural visions and values. The rigid education system and the snobbish mainstream culture have created indifference, cynicism and fear in our unconscious. We must try to expose ourselves to an environment filled with uncertainty, to seize every opportunity to shake up the habitual obstinacy and break out of the cage of constraint. It is not a shame to be "emotional"; on the contrary, the impact of emotions, stirring up ethical care and breaking through the so-called "rational" frame, can not only bring on a more profound understanding of things, but can also allow us to open all kinds of possibilities to cultivate perception, discernment, self-determination and the ability to act, to welcome an open life journey.

Knowing what is not possible and doing it: this is the perseverance and the audacity to do what should be done, and not to do what should not be done!

[This is introduction to the Chinese traditional character edition of the book published by Cosmos Books]

Notes

1. https://covid19.who.int/region/wpro/country/jp.
2. "Tokyo Olympics Most Expensive in History; International Olympics the Biggest Winner", August 7, 2021, Central News Agency, https://www.cna.com.tw/news/firstnews/202108070193.aspx.

3. From 2011 to 2021, Global University for Sustainability, Lingnan University, as well as a number of Chinese and overseas high education institutions have co-organized eight South-South forums, with the themes around alternative development, people's livelihoods, ecology, and sustainable culture. The Fukushima nuclear disaster has been at the forefront of ecological issues. Over the years, Ohashi Masaaki, Aihara Hiroko, Fujioka Emiko, and 2017 Nobel Peace Prize Laureate Rebecca Johnson, have continued making presentations at the South South Forum on Fukushima and global nuclear disasters. The full videos are available for free viewing at: https://our-global-u.org/oguorg/en/.
4. Lau Kin Chi, "Reflecting on Modern Education and Violence from the Perspective of Ecological Justice," in *Critical Teaching Encountering New Generation of Youths: A Study of Education in Mainland, Hong Kong and Taiwan*, edited by PK Hui, City University of Hong Kong Press, 2018, pp. 179–d197.

3

Introduction: When We Talk About Nuclear Energy, What Are We Talking About? Huang Xiaomei

In June 2019, the Sixth South-South Forum on Sustainability organized by the Global University for Sustainability invited Dr. Rebecca Johnson, Founding Co-Chair of the International Campaign to Abolish Nuclear Weapons, the Nobel Peace Prize Laureate of 2017, to hold a three-day summer camp in Hong Kong. The theme was "Nuclear Weapons and Power, Current Challenges and Responses". Professor Lau Kin Chi honored me with the assignment of simultaneous interpretation for the Chinese audience during the camp. I am an Arts graduate, a literary youth to the core. My scientific knowledge, even on such things as electricity generation, is no more than scanty. Seriously, by the end of the several days in the camp, I had learnt how nuclear bombs were made.

Later, in the course of collecting material for this book, I had watched the film *Homeland*, and cried a lot—being a literary youth as I have said. When I watched *Pandora* earlier, another film of a similar theme,

K. C. Lau et al., *The Fukushima Catastrophe*, Global University for Sustainability Book Series, https://doi.org/10.1007/978-981-99-1956-7_3

I had also cried despite knowing full well that it was Korean style sensationalism. However, the two kinds of feeling were not the same. What pervades in *Homeland* is the sense of attachment to every tree, every flower in the homeland, the sense of helplessness of individuals being whirled around in the catastrophe, forced into personal resistance even though knowing it would be to no avail. In *Pandora*, it was sensationalism embodied in bondages to loved ones amidst the crisis in the country.

The nuclear bomb with its impersonal coldness and the nuclear energy disaster with its human tragedies are not as far away from us as I had imagined. In fact, they are very, very close.

This book asks the readers "Do you remember what you did on that day, 11 March 2011?" I really have no recollection myself. At that time I was a student in Nanjing University. As that date was in the spring season, given the trait of a literary youth, I suppose I would have been reading a book under a tree. I had no memory of my reactions upon hearing this explosive piece of news. I was already a university student, yet was so ignorant. One thing is sure—I would not have any ideas back then that ten years later we would still be entwined with this issue, that we would still be plagued by the aftermaths, and that we would still need to make concerted efforts to convince people, rationally and emotionally, that nuclear energy is a no-go.

It seems quite obvious: nuclear energy is inefficient, radioactivity is dangerous, and the aftermaths of nuclear accidents are impossible to deal with. Who would be crazy enough to develop nuclear power? But indeed, there are such crazy people, and not too few in number.

I could not remember where I read the following episode, one that has remained in my mind ever since: in an anti-nuclear power seminar, a child said to all the adults "You are all hypocrites! You know very well that in future we have to face the problem of nuclear spent fuel, yet you continue to indulge in the use of energy from nuclear power plants!" Yes, on the issue of nuclear energy, it is a crime to keep silent. As such it is necessary to have this book telling readers what had happened and why.

I am obliged to Professor Lau Kin Chi for this opportunity to reflect on and to learn about this issue. I hope everyone who reads it will find it helpful.

4

Introduction: We Are in a Critical State—He Zhixiong

The earthquake and tsunami in Japan on March 11, 2011 had happened ten years ago, yet the aftermath of the Fukushima nuclear crisis is far from being over. As ordinary people who live far away from the core zone of the disaster, and not having been much impacted, it is easy for us to forget and neglect, with the notion that since it is no longer reported in the media it must have been over and done with. Yet when I came in touch with the related material from Japanese friends and began to look into it, I started to realize we common people are indeed simplistic in our understanding of the nuclear issue. Before then, I had not regarded nuclear crisis as an issue, thinking that even in case anything happens all that requires to be done is to close down the nuclear power plant.

Having been trained as a science student and ingrained in scientific and technological thinking, my interest is to investigate the horrors of nuclear crisis from a technological stance. People should realize that the decommissioning of a nuclear reactor in a nuclear power plant requires a process; it is not just the pressing of a button. Even in normal decommissioning, nuclear fission reactions would not stop completely. The reactor core will continue to generate heat. If the cumulative heat reaches a

K. C. Lau et al., *The Fukushima Catastrophe*, Global University for Sustainability Book Series, https://doi.org/10.1007/978-981-99-1956-7_4

certain critical temperature, nuclear reactions will erupt again. That is why after decommissioning, a cooling system is still needed to keep the reactor at a low-temperate state, so that it would not gradually overheat and cause a serious accident such as reactor core melt-down. The Japanese are reputed to be among the most disciplined and meticulous people in the world, yet in face of this nuclear crisis their handling had been in total disarray, committing one error after another. It shows clearly the enormous potential risk to human beings in the use of nuclear power, and the uncontrollable nature of what might happen during a nuclear mishap.

The reactor cores in Fukushima Nuclear Power Plant had experienced melt-down during the nuclear crisis. It is still unclear where that large quantity of nuclear fuel debris is, what condition it is in, and whether there would be nuclear critical reactions. The huge quantity of debris from the tsunami could only be cleared at a very slow pace given the concern of radiation contamination. Enormous amounts of nuclear contaminated water are still being produced in the process of cooling the reactors, and soon there would not be enough water storage containers. What should be done then? The quantity of contaminated soil and other debris collected in the process of decontamination is so huge that there is nowhere to put them. Decontamination sounds good in words but in fact it is impossible to completely get rid of the contamination. In most cases it is simply a matter of moving the contaminated material around. Further, the process of collecting and moving the debris might heighten the possibility of radiation exposure. The danger is far from being over.

Just as the Chernobyl accident in 1986 that gave rise to profound consequences, likewise the Fukushima accident's aftermaths are beginning to emerge. It is not expected to be resolved even over a very long run. What this means is that the lives of a large number of people will continue to be impacted. They may be discriminated against for fear of radiation exposure, they may suffer radiation sickness, or they may encounter the hardship of resettlement…

Perhaps it can be said that the critical state has already become normality in the lives of those in Eastern Japan—they can at any time be drawn from a "normal life" into the abnormality caused by nuclear contamination. As such they are forced to take extreme care in selecting food, to change their lifestyle so as to reduce the damage. The "critical state" is originally a concept in the nuclear reaction process, yet here it can be applied quite precisely to describe the state of people's lives under the impact of the mishap. It is critical because they are living continuously in a dynamic, the nature of which could change at any time. They cannot set their targets and future paths in accordance with any conventional logic.

The Tokyo Olympics was postponed from 2020 to 2021 due to the Covid-19 pandemic. In this regard the Japanese media had strived to create a scene of national joy. When they tried, quite successfully, to connect the spirit of the Olympic Games—mutual understanding, friendship, teamwork, fair competition—to Fukushima, they were in fact attempting to shroud the nuclear crisis there. The Japanese elites, through control of the media, have continuously propagated the myth of nuclear safety, or attempted to dilute the crisis to avoid taking action and taking accountability over what happened. The Tokyo Electric Power Company (TEPCO) and the government departments concerned have done no more than making cash settlement for legal cases filed by the victims. They have not been able to effectively handle the decontamination that is still on-going. People are concerned and angry, a stronger civil society anti-nuclear movement is growing, with frequent demonstrations against nuclear power.

This nuclear crisis is far from over and many dangers persist. People should not forget the truth behind the accident, the accountability, as well as the history of Japan's nuclear crises.

The publication of this book is intended to give readers a deeper understanding of the severity of the accident, thereby learning the lessons and grasping some basic knowledge on protection against nuclear contamination. After all, each and every one of us living in modern civilization is not far off from nuclear issues.

5

What Happened in Fukushima?

For most people, Friday, 11 March 2011, was just any other day with nothing particularly noteworthy. Babies born, people passing away—these happen every day. Yet in the northeastern part of Japan, an unprecedented powerful earthquake erupted. At a magnitude of 9.0 on the Richter scale, it gave rise to the largest tsunami ever recorded in Japan. In face of that mighty force of nature, humans were no match. Worse, the Fukushima Daiichi Nuclear Power Plant, located in the town of Okuma in Fukushima Prefecture, was hit by a 15-meter tsunami that had broken through the embankment, with the result that both the normal power supply and the backup power generators failed to operate. What followed was failure of the cooling system, and then like dominos, one piece relentlessly collapsed after another.

K. C. Lau et al., *The Fukushima Catastrophe*, Global University for Sustainability Book Series, https://doi.org/10.1007/978-981-99-1956-7_5

A view of the decommissioned Fukushima Daiichi Nuclear Power Plant from the mountain in Okuma, April 2018. (Photo by Aihara Hiroko)

The life trajectory of those who lived along the northeastern coast of Japan has been completely changed since then. The clock at the nuclear plant site would forever stop at that moment, because the future would not be arriving.

The nuclear power plant's design did of course come with safety mechanisms. When the earthquake erupted, it was detected by sensors. The safety system was triggered as designed to stop reactors number 1 to 3 that were operating at the time. Yet even after the nuclear reactors stopped, their cores would continue to generate heat (called decay heat), and under normal circumstances a cooling system would come into operation to reduce their temperature. Yet that day was anything but normal circumstances. The most direct alternative was to inject water from outside into the reactor cores.

Imagine that moment. With the earthquake and tsunami happening, the nuclear power plant that usually operated in an orderly manner was in complete chaos. The debris brought in by the seawater had settled everywhere. Lids were flushed off ditches and there were holes on the ground all over. Both inside the plant and out on the roads, the ground had been elevated in some parts and sunken in others. It became hazardous to enter the plant or to go around inside. Emergency response measures were wrought with difficulty at every step, figuratively and literally, and continuously interrupted by aftershocks. Without power supply it also meant that the monitoring system could not operate, and in turn the control room's function also failed. Lighting and communication were also affected. Everything fell back upon manual operation. Was there a procedure set out in the 'Safety Manual' (if there was such a thing) for that kind of situation? Not really! Those on the ground could only work 'in the dark'. And time meant lives.

It was 17.5 hours after the power supply failure that a pipe was finally set up to start injecting water from the fire water tank into the core of Reactor No. 1. However, the water was used up after only 11 hours. Readers might ask, since Fukushima Nuclear Power Plant was right by the sea, why not use seawater? Those on the ground obviously had thought of this most direct water source, and in fact had completed the set-up for seawater injection within half an hour. Yet it was not put into use right away, but 4 hours later.[1] It was suggested afterwards that the reason was the reluctance of TEPCO, owner of the nuclear power plant, to use untreated seawater, as that would render the reactor permanently non-operational and require it to be scrapped.

What is the consequence of not cooling the reactor core? Not having water circulating and cooling down the temperature continuously, the fuel rods inside the reactor core would quickly heat up and evaporate the water that is there (the temperature at the center of the fuel rod is 2800 degrees Celsius). The fuel rods would begin to melt, causing the reactor core to melt down, and melting the bottom of the pressure vessel as well as possibly the external protective shell. Radiation leaked and an environmental catastrophe would occur. It was a choice of priority between the prevention of radiation contamination of the environment and the consideration of TEPCO's economic interest. Looking at it in hindsight, the choice being made then was reprehensible.

Damage to the Fukushima Daiichi Nuclear Power Plant in 2011, courtesy of the Japan NGO Center for International Cooperation (JANIC). (Photo by Fujioka Emiko)

Likewise for Reactor number 2, after ascertaining that it had also lost the cooling function, management personnel on the ground had attempted to inject seawater using the firefighting system. Yet the pressure within the reactor was too high for the fire engine pumps to be able to inject water into it. The decision was then made to reduce the pressure inside the reactor with the relief valves. Yet the side effect of that was weakening the sealing tightness of the reactor. Further, since ventilation for the reactor could not be successfully set up, pressure inside the protective capsule also kept on rising and seriously affecting water injection. On March 15, an explosion erupted and the pressure readings of the protective capsule started to decline. It was an indication that the capsule could have become dysfunctional and radioactive material was leaking.

It was later disclosed that injection of cooling water into the reactor had been disrupted for more than 6 hours.[2]

As for Reactor Number 3, it also lost the cooling function. A pipe to inject seawater was readily completed within one hour. Yet there were different stories as to whether seawater had been immediately used. The more credible version was the one given in the official report issued by the Fukushima Nuclear Accident Independent Investigation Commission in 2012. It was said that although TEPCO's head office had ordered Mr. Yoshida, head of the nuclear plant, not to use seawater, the latter disobeyed, albeit not openly. That wise decision of Yoshida might have averted a worse disaster. One thing was sure, the top priority of TEPCO's senior management had been economic interests.

There were altogether six reactors in Fukushima Daiichi Nuclear Power Plant. Number 1 and 3 were in operation on the day of March 11, 2011. Their essential safety functions were either seriously impaired or completely lost, ending with the worst kind of nuclear disaster - meltdown of the reactor core. It was two months later in May 2011 that TEPCO acknowledged there had been a meltdown. Prior to that the company had simply said there was no basis to assess whether that had happened. The intention was to hide or dilute the seriousness of the accident. The 'Nuclear Disaster Response Manual' kept at TEPCO's head office clearly states that if more than 5% of the reactor core is damaged, it should be assessed as a meltdown. As such TEPCO did have a basis for assessment, and on that basis, it should have said that there had been a meltdown on the fourth day, 14 March. It was five years later, in a press conference on 30 May 2016, that TEPCO finally admitted to having concealed the facts, and offered an apology.

So, the worst happened: a nuclear core meltdown. What were the implications?

The meltdown could have damaged the bottom wall of the reactor, and debris of the molten nuclear fuel rods could have fallen off and gradually seeped into the ground to contaminate the underground water. At the end of May 2011, experts from the investigation team of the International Atomic Energy Agency (IAEA) issued a report, pointing out that the molten fuel rods of Reactors 1 to 3 did fall off. Part of it had likely melted through the pressure vessel, accumulated at the bottom of the protective capsule, and melted through it also. Even today, more than ten years later, no one knows the exact positions of the holes that had been made. Neither does anyone know how much melted radioactive material there was. No one has ever anticipated an accident like this ever occurring.

When all this was happening in the nuclear power plant, in a scene out of a disaster movie, those people who were suffering the double onslaught of the earthquake and tsunami did not realize that the curtain was just being raised on their calamity.

Notes

1. International Atomic Energy Agency (IAEA) "The Fukushima Daiichi Accident: Report by the Director General", 2015.
2. "Reactors Number 2 and 3 of Fukushima Nuclear Power Plant in Japan may be melting down", https://www.china-nea.cn/site/content/19240.html.

6

Natural Disasters or Human-Caused Calamity

It was "unexpected" that there would be a 15-meter tsunami—so the embankment was only built to the height of 5.7 meters.

It was "unexpected" that the power supply system and the backup diesel-fueled power generators in the nuclear power plant would fail at the same time—as such nothing could be done when it happened.

It was "unexpected" that the so-called 'emergency automatic cooler' was of little help—as such the reactor core meltdown had happened after all.

It was "unexpected" ……

It was "unexpected" that the Japanese people, globally renowned for their craftsmanship and sophisticated technology, were not able to adopt the necessary response measures when the Fukushima Nuclear Power Plant was hit by this natural disaster. It was "unexpected" that the Japanese government, famous for its efficiency, and having made the claim that nuclear power was absolutely safe, could do nothing to stop the disaster from escalating, to stop the radiation leakage that resulted in 140,000[1] people losing their homes, the contamination of the

K. C. Lau et al., *The Fukushima Catastrophe*, Global University for Sustainability Book Series, https://doi.org/10.1007/978-981-99-1956-7_6

coastal regions, and the spread of contamination possibly to other countries. The countless "unexpected" developments have cumulated into an irremediable catastrophe.

Yet, while all those developments may have been "unexpected", they were certainly not "beyond expectation".

In June 2012, the Nuclear Accident Independent Investigation Commission published an official report on the Fukushima disaster. It pointed out clearly that the accident was human-caused, and the reason was that sections of the Japanese governments as well as TEPCO's management lacked a sense of responsibility in protecting people's lives and safeguarding the public.[2]

Based on their investigation, the Commission indicated that as of 11 March 2011, the Fukushima Daiichi Power Plant was not equipped or capable of being properly safeguarded against earthquakes and tsunamis, and up to that point in time had not taken measures that should have been undertaken in that regard.[3] In 2006, the standards to guard against earthquakes were revised. Not only did TEPCO fail to strengthen the safety of the reactors accordingly, it had also postponed the scheduled seismic inspection from 2009 to 2016. As it turned out, that was too late. What is more terrifying is that, according to the report, as early as 2006 both the Nuclear and Industrial Safety Agency and TEPCO already had the understanding that in the case of a tsunami higher than the power plant, all power supplies would fail. The risk of reactor core damage was known to them. Yet the Agency accepted TEPCO's do-nothing strategy and did not make any demands on the company.[4]

That is to say, all of those 'unexpected' circumstances had been predicted well beforehand. Yet the nuclear power plant's safety guidelines did not give any consideration to the possibility of complete power failure, nor did it mention the possibility of such a tsunami, because those in charge dismissed the possibility as low. What seemed chilling was that such 'ominous' terms like tsunami, earthquake, power failure, and so on, were treated as taboo in Japan's "nuclear power arena", and as such were not listed for consideration.[5]

Back in 1995, on 17 January, a Richter scale 7.3 earthquake erupted in the Osaka-Kobe area. In the following month, a seminar was held in Osaka to oppose the launch of the Monju prototype fast breeder reactor.[6] During the discussions the people asked what would happen to the Monju reactor if an earthquake similar to that in Osaka-Kobe was to occur. The officials' reply was that such an earthquake would not happen there. From that one could glimpse the mentality of those in charge.

Nature 'deliberately' played a joke to ridicule the stupidity and arrogance of human beings. In 2008, the Japan Society of Civil Engineering's tsunami assessment committee, based on a long-term projection calculation, had assessed that the Fukushima nuclear power plant might be hit by a 15-meter tsunami. Yet, TEPCO's senior management felt long-term assessments were based on assumed figures and decided not to spend four years as well as tens of billions of yen to build a 15-meter breakwater. By comparison, in September 2010, the Tokai Nuclear Power Plant in neighboring Iberaki, had heightened its breakwater from 4.9 meters to 6.1 meters. During the 11 March 2011 incident, the tsunami at Iberaki reached 5.4 meters, and the plant was able to narrowly escape a catastrophe![7]

The disaster scene at Fukushima Daiichi Nuclear Power Plant was complete chaos.

There hadn't been a similar situation before. The emergency system had not given an alarm in forty years. Even when the system ejected large quantities of steam, it did not immediately occur to the staff that there was a problem with the reactor.

The first emergency power supply vehicle that TEPCO sent could not reach the plant due to traffic congestion. The second one arrived at 11 pm that night but could not be readily connected to the reactor because the cable was not long enough. After much effort it was finally connected but it was then discovered that the voltage was not compatible with the reactor's requirement, and there was no transformer. Batteries were requested, yet what came was the wrong model. The staff then used the batteries removed from vehicles on site, taking a lot of time to do that.

The senior management of TEPCO insisted on injecting fresh water to the reactors so that the reactors might still be usable later, yet fresh water supply was simply not sufficient. The staff phoned for 4000 tonnes of fresh water yet what they received was 4000 liters!

It was necessary to open the exhaust valves to release the pressure inside the safety capsule in order to avoid a hydrogen explosion. As power was lost it had to be done by hand. Then it was discovered that the operating manual did not have instructions on that manual process. The staff thought of studying the design drawings to find out how it could be done, yet the drawings were not readily found and they had to look around for them. This sounds absurd yet this is what happened.

With the findings that TEPCO had information in their possession regarding the risk and vulnerability of the Daiichi power plant yet had delayed corrective measures and neglected emergency response preparedness, the investigation commission concluded that the accident was not the problem of individual operational staff, but the problem of the TEPCO management.[8]

TEPCO had blundered from the very beginning. After the earthquake, it did not communicate first-hand the news about failure of the cooling system. When Reactor Number 1 exploded on 12 March TEPCO again did not report it first-hand to the Japanese authorities. Even the Prime Minister had found out only through television reporting and it was an hour later that the report arrived at his office. Moreover, in handling the crisis, TEPCO did not make it a priority to prevent a nuclear disaster, in not immediately authorizing the use of seawater to cool the reactor cores. The time delays and chaotic responses had meant losing any chance of averting the core meltdowns, and the consequence was an even more serious ecological catastrophe.[9]

The human errors described above were on the technical and organizational front. These were just the superficial, direct causes. If not in Fukushima, that accident could have happened in any other nuclear power plant in Japan. What this accident has exposed are some deeply buried issues in the development of nuclear power in Japan.

Notes

1. Aihara Keiko "Eight Years since the Fukushima Accident: Current Situation and Issues in Fukushima", Chinese translation by Kelven Cheung; Aihara Keiko was born in Fukushima Township about 65 km from the Fukushima Nuclear Power Plant explosion zone.
2. *Foreign Nuclear Power* Journal, 2012 Issue No. 5, translated by Wang Shengguo.
3. Ditto.
4. Ditto.
5. Chen Hongmei: *Japan 3.11 Apocalypse.*
6. Monju Reactor had not been given protection by its patron God Bodhisattva Manjusri and had suffered many setbacks. Since construction started in 1970, more than 1 trillion Yen had been spent on it. Yet because of numerous accidents, the Japanese government decided to decommission it in December 2016. It was in operation for a total of merely 250 days. Moreover, tragic suicide cases had happened in two of the accidents, in one case an investigator of the accident and in the other the person accountable for the accident.
7. Li Yuan, Wang Xuan: "Lies and Arrogance: The Truth of Nuclear Disasters in Japan".
8. *Foreign Nuclear Power Journal*, 2012 Issue No. 5, translated by Wang Shengguo.
9. "Tokyo Electric Power Company accused of 'six deadly sins' in manipulating data to conceal accidents" *Guangzhou Daily*, April 10, 2011.

7

Fairy Tale of Astro Boy

A view of Fukushima Daiichi Nuclear Power Plant from Okuma in 2018, courtesy of Fukushima Beacon for Global Citizens Network (FUKUDEN). (Photo by Fujioka Emiko)

K. C. Lau et al., *The Fukushima Catastrophe*,
Global University for Sustainability Book Series,
https://doi.org/10.1007/978-981-99-1956-7_7

The official report of the Fukushima Nuclear Accident Independent Investigation Commission clearly pointed out that "The underlying issue is the social structure that results in 'regulatory capture', and the organizational, institutional, and legal framework that allows individuals to justify their own actions, conceal them when inconvenient, and leave no records in order to avoid responsibility… We found an organization-driven mindset that prioritized benefits to the organization at the expense of the public."[1]

The report further indicated that there was an even bigger body of 'common interest' centering around 'regulatory capture', including nuclear power manufacturers, the Ministry of Economy and Industry, the Ministry of Culture and Science, the media, mainstream academics, and so on—groups that would benefit from promoting nuclear power. This interest bloc has exerted significant influence on the political, financial, academic, and mass media arenas.

The Fukushima nuclear power plant is the case in point.

It was one of the largest of its kind in the world. The power it generated was not for local usage supply but transmitted to the Tokyo area two hundred kilometers away. In 1960, when the plan for Fukushima Daiichi nuclear power plant was announced, the local government welcomed it with the belief that it would attract other industries to the area and stimulate the local economy. TEPCO had involved the local authorities and government personnel in negotiations over the relevant issues such as land acquisition, compensation to the fishery industry and so on. The 2014 Japanese film *Homeland* is a poetic disaster story about an ordinary Fukushima family after the nuclear accident. The main character's deceased father was a candidate for town council, whose election slogan had been the promotion of nuclear power. TEPCO had even dealt with land acquisition using gangsters, as one gang leader blatantly admitted to Tomohiko Suzuki, a writer who slipped inside the nuclear power plant to conduct investigations.[2] Concerns and objections of the local people had been drowned out by assurances that radioactive rays were neither dangerous nor harmful.

Moreover, in 1974 the Japanese government introduced the new laws known as Three Power Source Laws, providing for enormous amounts of subsidies and fixed asset taxation payments to local authorities as compensation for taking on the risk of nuclear power plants. Such payments have been used towards building glittering public infrastructures and did appear to have boosted local economic development for a short span of time. However, twenty years after the time of construction, the subsidies and tax revenues have become much lower. To maintain the public infrastructures, local authorities have fallen into the quagmire of relying on new nuclear power plant constructions.[3]

The unanimous support for nuclear power during the 1960s among the government, TEPCO and the mass media had much to do with their respective self-interests. Government officials, after retirement, have the common practice of moving to nominal yet well-paid positions in private corporations. TEPCO is one of those corporations well-versed in this practice. In a survey conducted in 2011, it was found that in the preceding 50 years TEPCO had employed a total of 68 retired senior-level bureaucrats from the Ministry of Economy and Industry.[4] Members of Congress, regardless of party affiliation, have connections to the nuclear power field. Nuclear power becomes the wallet for politicians, and the national strategy on nuclear power is the outcome of mutual benefits between them and the nuclear power field.

The pricing of electric power is by law to be established on a cost-based approach. If the cost increases, the price will be revised upward accordingly. Although the costs of nuclear power construction are high, the utility sector is still assured of a stable profit. Further, the high construction costs have provided profits to construction companies, which in turn given the banks a stream of stable and safe profit by taking out loans to finance the construction. Electricity companies, construction companies and banks thus formed a body of mutual benefits centering on nuclear power construction. In the financial sector, electric power companies are bellwethers, able to exert tremendous impact on the market. Their shareholders are composed mainly of insurance companies, banks, governments, and large enterprises. Only about 10% of the shareholders are individuals. TEPCO is without doubt a giant enterprise, with operations all the way from power generation to transmission to distribution. With market value of around 14 trillion Yen and a staff of over 40,000, TEPCO is known to be the world's biggest private-run nuclear power company.

In the academic realm, the universities that should have been the ones to protect those with no attachments to politics and power, yet welcomed those scholars who support nuclear power and suppressed those with opposing views. That is because those in support of nuclear power would bring in large sums of project research funds. The Japanese magazine *Bessatsu Takarajima* once published a list of nuclear power organization fundings to professors in national universities around the country, and the amounts had been from millions of yens to tens of millions.[5] On the other hand, Assistant Professor Hiroaki Koide in Kyoto University, with his firm stance against nuclear power, was not promoted to Professorship even at retirement after 45 years. His anti-nuclear books were rarely heard of before 11 March 2011 but have become bestsellers since.

In the mass media field, the government has been funding 300 million Yen annually to the Japan Atomic Energy Culture Foundation, an organization that promotes the safety of nuclear power and fosters the nuclear fairy tale. This organization would spend 1 billion Yen every year to promote nuclear power through scholars and popular entertainers. Electricity companies also invest huge sums on advertisements to promote the message of nuclear power's absolute safety (before the accident, TEPCO had spent 50 billion Yen every year on this).[6] Given that the profit of electricity companies in Japan is assured on a cost-plus basis, the higher the advertising expense, the higher the profit for the companies. Thus, with the power companies becoming their key customers, newspapers and television stations are not in the position to say 'no' to the nuclear safety propaganda.

The media blocks the discourse of anti-nuclear scholars. They also ban actors and singers with anti-nuclear messages. Not doing so would affect their business. For example, *Tokyo Shimbun* had made blatant and sharply critical comments against nuclear power after the Fukushima accident, and many enterprises took their advertisements off that paper.

The Japanese nuclear bloc has not been restrained even after the Fukushima accident. Prime Minister Naoto Kan did make two alternative proposals for reforming the nuclear power sector, in an attempt to weaken the latter's influence. The first proposal was for electricity companies to diversify the sources of electricity by buying from people who generate electricity using alternative power source such as solar and wind. The second proposal was to segregate the generation and the transmission of electricity, giving other enterprises the usage rights of transmission networks and infrastructures. Ultimately, the first proposal was passed in exchange for the Prime Minister himself to step down. Further, the Nuclear Safety Agency was transferred from the Ministry of Economy, Trade, and Industry to the Ministry of Environment, thus severing its ties with past collusions. Yet after Prime Minister Shinzo Abe came on board, firm government support for the nuclear bloc was revived.

It was ironical that Japan, the only country in the world that had suffered atomic bombing, would be where nuclear power was successfully introduced in the 1950s-1970s, and from which nuclear power has spread to the rest of the world. In this process the government and the media played a pivotal role. The development of nuclear power in Japan was driven by the U.S., the country that had dropped atomic bombs to Hiroshima and Nagasaki. In the 1950s, the U.S. had conducted massive campaigns to promote the "peaceful use of nuclear power" through *Yomiuri Shimbun*, the newspaper with top circulation in Japan, thereby changing the views of the Japanese people towards nuclear power.

Over the decades, with all sorts of speeches, study programs, propaganda and school visits, people began to be convinced in the safety of nuclear power. In Hiroshima's Atomic Bomb Museum Building, right next to the exhibition hall dedicated to the devastation of the atomic bomb, is the display hall for materials on the peaceful use of nuclear energy.[7] Some of those who joined nuclear power plant constructions in the early days had been from Hiroshima and had lived through the atomic bombing. They were confident and enthusiastic, convinced by the propaganda message and looked upon it as the 'job for real men'.[8]

Astro Boy, a comics character created in the 1960s that has remained popular to this day, still raises his right hand in the fight for future good of humanity. It was fun to watch him as a child, not knowing that he was in fact closely linked to the strategy of developing 'peaceful use of nuclear power'. The name "Astro" had actually come from the word "Atom". In the Astro Boy comics, Astro has a younger sister "Uran". While she was not as famous, her name was just as fierce, having been derived from the word "Uranium", the fuel for generating nuclear power or making nuclear bomb. This kind of invisible brainwashing is even more persuasive than direct propaganda, and more terrifying. When nuclear accidents first started to happen, the local people did not treat it seriously because they had the firm belief that such "high-tech" facilities would be fool proofed against natural disasters like earthquakes and tsunami. Even if there were problems, they had faith in the government and the experts to resolve them, so grandiose and convincing the latter's narratives had been. Little did they know that the experts and the government were speaking either out of self-interest or out of ignorance.

So, in this fairy tale that is created—that nuclear power was more environment-friendly, safer, and more cost effective—where are the tricks that have fooled people into believing?

Notes

1. "Tokyo Electric Power Company accused of 'six deadly sins' in manipulating data to conceal accidents", *Guangzhou Daily*, April 10, 2011.
2. "Fukushima 50, the tragic cost of the employees", HK01, June 24, 2020.
3. *10 Lessons from Fukushima—Reducing risks and protecting communities from nuclear disasters*, Fukushima Booklet Committee.
4. Zhou Qi, executive director of National Institute of strategic studies, Tsinghua University "Is Tokyo Electric Power Company simply a business?" *Guancha*, March 29, 2013.
5. Chen Hungmei: *Japan 3.11 Apocalypse.*
6. *10 Lessons from Fukushima—Reducing risks and protecting communities from nuclear disasters*, Fukushima Booklet Committee.
7. Muto Ichiyo: "Potential Nuclear Ownership and Post-war States".
8. "Our Islands: from Hiroshima to Fukushima", *Public Television Service* (Taiwan PTS), September 19, 2011.

8

Three Questions on Nuclear Power

We often come across the argument that one should not give up eating for the fear of choking. Obviously, we should not reject nuclear power just because of "one accident". Having said that, let us examine what kind of "food" nuclear power is, whether it is fit for "eating".

First Question: Is Nuclear Power Good for Environmental Protection?

Indeed, the process of generating electricity using nuclear power would not give rise to carbon dioxide. Yet, how about what happens before and after the generation process?

The generation of nuclear electricity starts with the mining of uranium, the logistics of which are: excavation- transportation- refining- enriching- processing- reactor building- reprocessing- transporting spent nuclear fuel- disposing spent nuclear fuel. Every step along the way involves the consumption of large quantity of oil fuel. Nuclear electricity is no more than a converted form of fossil fuel.[1] In particular, building

K. C. Lau et al., *The Fukushima Catastrophe*, Global University for Sustainability Book Series, https://doi.org/10.1007/978-981-99-1956-7_8

a nuclear electricity power plant requires building thick concrete walls reinforced with steel bars. When it is de-commissioned, it becomes a completely useless and radioactive site. Dismantling it not only requires even more human-power and material than the original construction, it is also impossible to avoid radiation exposure. Up to mid-2019, among the 181 nuclear reactors that were shut down in the world, only 19 had been completely de-commissioned. Of these, only 10 could achieve the threshold standard for "developable land". Even for these limited cases, the uncertainty level was as high as 20%.[2] The simplest disposal method for scrapped nuclear power plants that the intelligent humans could come up with to date, is to cover the site, bury it in a huge "concrete tomb". Yet building the concrete tomb requires oil fuel also, and that emits carbon dioxide. Further, the concrete tomb is not a once-and-for-all effort. It needs regular maintenance. At the end of the day, the quantity of energy being used far exceeds that which the nuclear power plant generates.

While operation of the nuclear power plant itself does not generate carbon dioxide, it does generate radiation contaminated substances, such as the exhaust gas that continuously emits from the tall exhaust pipes, as well as the cooling water from the reactor. The quantity of cooling water needed is huge, and it cannot be recycled after use. That is why nuclear power plants are usually built by the sea or river. Seawater is regarded as 'inexhaustible'. During normal operation, tens of tonnes of hot wastewater would be emitted to the sea every minute.[3] In addition, the water being used to wash the personal protective wears of workers is also disposed into the sea. The radiation level is outrageously high in areas where the wastewater is disposed, yet fishermen could be breeding fish in the area without knowing about it.[4]

What is more important to consider is the disposal of the large quantity of spent nuclear fuel. It is a nightmare that will remain in the human world over tens of thousands of years. According to statistics from the World Nuclear Association (WNA), up to the end of 2013 there was a total of 250,000 tons of highly radioactive nuclear spent fuel awaiting further handling, and with every year that passed there would be an increase of 10,000 tons. In Japan's nuclear power plants, all spent fuel is "temporarily" stored in the cooling tank at the upper part of the reactor.

The potential risk for leakage is severe. For example, in August 2005, a Richter scale 7.2 earthquake had led to overflowing of the cooling water from the cooling tanks in Fukushima Daiichi and Fukushima II Nuclear Power Plants.

After completion of the cooling process that would take decades, part of the spent fuel can be reused, and the rest is disposed of by the temporary burial approach. Finding a burial site is a big problem, and after the burial there are bigger problems left for the future posterity to handle. In the meantime, these problematic rubbish and wastes are kept out of the sight of our own generation so we can continue to enjoy the comfort of our lives.

After the Fukushima accident, Germany made the decision to close down all nuclear power plants by 2022. The predicament is how to bury the highly radioactive spent fuel. At present, Germany has 2000 containers for storing the spent fuel. There are three main problems.

First, how to find an underground site to bury the spent fuel permanently and safely, a place where earthquakes or water seepage would not occur. In one case, a former salt mine used for nuclear spent fuel storage has been regularly soaked by in-flow of surface water. The mixture of spent fuel and salt, a volume of 220,000 cubic meters, needs urgent handling. It is not only complex but also very expensive.[5] The second problem is how the spent fuel can be safely shipped to the designated site. And the third, how to pass on to future humankind the information regarding potential risks.

All these problems are saying, once again, that at present humans do not have the capability needed to use nuclear power. The third problem is particularly embarrassing: how do we tell our future generations that the estate left by their ancestors is the highly radioactive material that the ancestors did not know how to handle, something that may need 100,000 years to resolve? Of all the magnificent structures and spectacular sights in the world, how many of them can last 10,000 years, 50,000 years, 100,000 years? By then, multiple civilizations could have already come and faded out. Yet that highly radioactive material would remain a danger.

To be truly environmentally friendly, it is necessary to start by reducing energy usage through changing the consumerist lifestyle, not self-contradictorily encouraging the use of another energy form.

Entrance of Fukushima Daiichi Nuclear Power Plant (Photo by Ohashi Masaaki)

Second Question: Is Nuclear Power Safe?

On this question, the Fukushima disaster has given an obvious answer. Nuclear power is not simply power, it is nuclear. 'Nuclear safety' is an oxymoron. Where there is nuclear there would be no safety but risk. The so-called 'safety' is no more than a beautiful bubble created by governments, producers, and nuclear power company experts, based on data skewed to their stance.

View of Fukushima Daiichi Nuclear Power Plant (Photo by Ohashi Masaaki)

The Fukushima power plant was built to withstand Richter scale 7 earthquakes. Yet on 11 March 2011, what had erupted was level 9. Can we say, then, that at fault was not the design of the plant but the earthquake itself? Can anyone guarantee that the next earthquake would not be level 9 + ? We cannot predict when and where natural disasters would happen. We simply know that they will happen. At this time, with human beings barely able to manage nuclear power or natural forces such as the shifting of Tectonic Plates, humankind have no one to blame but themselves when catastrophes such as that in Fukushima happen.

The radiation level was very high near the Fukushima Daiichi Nuclear Power Plant. (Photo by Ohashi Masaaki)

Even if we can ignore the factor of Nature, we cannot rule out human errors. The more complex the system, the more error-prone, the harder to recover, and the more deadly. There has been no lack of "minor" errors in the construction of nuclear power plants, many of which were not uncovered until long afterwards. Such incidents have resulted in deviations of the plants from their original designs, and the consequence is anyone's guess. There are simply two few experienced and well-trained workers in the field. Training someone on site is very difficult. The working conditions are harsh. Workers must wear protective gears which make it difficult for them to directly communicate with one another. Moreover, those more experienced workers would have been inside the high-contaminated area in more instances. They would have to be taken off their jobs as soon as their radiation exposure level exceeds the limit. Thus the work force as a whole is increasingly inexperienced.

The damage of nuclear disaster in Miyagi Prefecture, 2011. (Photo by Ohashi Masaaki)

Jinzaburo Takagi, a Japanese nuclear power expert and an anti-nuclear activist, had come across many of these problems. He cited examples from his personal experiences relating cases of serious problems arising from negligence, in turn due to objectives of cost reduction and profit allocation to different parties. One instance had to do with the manufacturing of ducts, which was assigned to different companies for production. However, these different companies had different practices of rounding-up, and as a result the respective parts produced could not be joined together. This was exactly what happened to the Monju Nuclear Reactor. Jinzaburo Takagi was the one being asked to investigate the problem. He studied the design layouts and discovered that it was co-designed by Hitachi, Toshiba, Mitsubishi and Fuji. Among them, Hitachi adopted a rounding up that cast away measurements smaller than 0.5 mm, while Toshiba and Mitsubishi included everything under 0.5 mm. The difference seemed trivial but it resulted in the parts being made by the different companies incompatible. The devil is in the details.

Radiation is an 'invisible killer' and once leakage occurs, it is quite impossible to contain. The radiation, being odorless, colorless, all-pervasive, can only be detected with instruments. After the Fukushima accident, "unexpected" radiation contamination was detected in one incidence after another. In one case, the beef produced at a distance of more than 170 kilometers away from Fukushima Nuclear Power Plant was found to have been contaminated. The source was determined to be the fodder that the cattle had fed on, with radiation level as high as 9000 becquerel (Bq). On further investigations regarding the cause of that high radiation level, it was found that the wind had blown in that direction on March 15, a spring day on which farmers were drying fodder under the sun.[6]

It was just 25 years after the Chernobyl accident when that tragic story was still being told, that another such story had taken place in human history. Do we want another Chernobyl, another Fukushima?[7]

Jinzaburo Takagi had predicted this kind of outcomes of the atomic age 24 years ago: due to on-going mismanagement and facility deterioration, when tsunami waves exceeding ten meters were to hit, all power sources would be lost, resulting in reactor core meltdown and serious radioactivity leakage.[8] It was not a fantasied disaster, but reality. Do we still want to cover our eyes and block our ears?

Third Question: Is Nuclear Power Cheap?

The cost effectiveness of nuclear electric power is only true for the power companies, as the bulk of the related cost falls on the government and the public.

First, the illusion of low cost has come about because power companies would only make public the obvious costs of uranium fuel and reactor operation. Other costs are being spent on an on-going basis for propaganda, education, and 'buying' the local people. Further, billions and tens of billions of yen in tax payments would have to be made to the selected site's local authorities.

Another major cost relates to disposing of the spent fuel and decommissioning obsolete reactors. The cost of completely decommissioning a reactor is outrageously high. In the United States, the cost varies between US$ 280 to US$ 1,500 per kilowatt. In Germany, it is US$ 1,900 per kilowatt. In comparison, the electricity charge in the U.S. in

March 2020 was US$ 0.147 per kilowatt hour, and in Germany in 2019, the charge was US$ 0.35 per kilowatt hour.[9]

The high costs of decommissioning obsolete reactors and handling spent fuel regularly have resulted in an "Energy Return on Energy Investment (EROEI)" that is as low as 4:1, meaning that 1 part of nuclear power would only generate 4 parts of energy. This is similar to that of wood burning. In comparison, coal has an EROEI of 10:1, while oil was previously 150:1 and coming down to 100:1 with the easily drillable oil wells exhausted.[10] It is no wonder that the U.S. anti-nuclear forerunner Michael Mariotte had written to *New York Times* in 2010 that there was no economic rationality to nuclear power generation.[11]

In principle, every country upholds the policy of having nuclear power operators accountable for managing, storing, and disposing spent nuclear fuel. Yet in practice, after the facilities are closed, operators would not be asked to take up financial responsibilities. The costs would be borne by taxpayers.

Regarding the Fukushima accident, the estimated budget for dealing with it was 22 trillion Yen, with the year 2050 as the end point. 16 trillion Yen would come from TEPCO (meaning that the electricity charge to residents would be rising), 2 trillion Yen to be borne by the Japanese government for decontamination, and the remaining costs would come from the electric power sector. That means even those consumers who choose a power supplier other than TEPCO would have to bear a share.[12]

It should be noted that the above budget is likely to have been underestimated. The Japanese Center for Economic Research (JCER) has made estimations based on different options. In their 2019 estimations, even the most basic option—not decommissioning the reactors, i.e., leaving the nuclear fuel inside the reactors, and emitting contaminated water into the ocean—was expected to cost 35 trillion Yen, while the best approach—decommissioning the reactors and not emitting contaminated water into the ocean—would cost 81 trillion Yen.

Regarding damage compensation, the Japanese government's priority has been to safeguard the survival of TEPCO, with the result that the government and other power companies have supplemented the inadequate compensation paid by TEPCO. Ultimately these costs would be transferred to the people at large through higher electricity charges and taxes.[13] TEPCO has even received capital financing of 1 trillion Yen from the government to help cover their damage.[14] All these costs will be borne by everyone in the country knowingly or unknowingly.

Are There No Alternatives to Supply Electricity Other Than Nuclear Power Generation?

Of course not. It is simply that the government does not want alternatives.

Before the Fukushima accident, the thermal power generation facilities in Japan were operating at only 50% capacity. Half of the capacity had been idle. In fact, if 20% more capacity was to be utilized, it would have been sufficient to replace the power generated by all of Japan's 54 nuclear generation units. Yet the nuclear power bloc did not agree to this. In the summer of 2011, with all nuclear power plants shut down after the accident, contrary to the expectation of power shortages there had been surplus power supply in places like Tokyo and Osaka. And in April 2012, the total electricity power generated in Japan was 102.7% of that in the same period in 2011. Of this, hydro power generation was 128% of that in same period 2011, thermal power generation 144.6% and nuclear power generation only 4%. That is to say, Japan can well live without nuclear power.

From August 2015 to September 2019, 9 nuclear power units were brought back into service. At present, power generation based on fossil fuel is still as high as 80% while nuclear power is only 3%. On 3 July 2018, the Japanese government put forward the "Fifth Strategic Energy Plan" in which the energy structure target is to be consisted of: "renewable energy 22–24%, nuclear 20–22%, thermal 56%". On this basis, there will be a need to activate more than 30 nuclear power units.[15]

Nuclear power is not good for the environment, not safe and not actually cheap. Yet because it is by nature obscure and closeted, it becomes an attractive profit-generation machine to the vested interest groups in the government and the nuclear power sector, one that is not subject to close monitoring. They want the nuclear power machines to keep on printing money for them, regardless of the potential risks. Professor Tian Song of Beijing Normal University concluded in his essay, "The Light of the Sun or the Fire of Purgatory", that the problem of nuclear power was not a problem of energy, but a problem of civilization—the problem of industrial civilization itself.[16] Another writer, Chen Hungmei, in her book "Japan's 3.11 Apocalypse", had also made this point. She said that the theory of nuclear power was very similar to the theory of financial game—using an extremely small quantity of uranium and causing it to multiply into an astronomical amount through repeated fissions. Not only are the theories similar. The development of nuclear power is also stimulated by capital, ballooning continuously until one day it would explode. Its destructive power, like the financial tsunami, will also be on an astronomical scale. Those who ultimately pay the biggest price are the millions and millions of common people.

Notes

1. Chen Hongmei: *Japan 3.11 Apocalypse.*
2. "The World Nuclear Waste Report 2019", Heinrich Böll Stiftung (HBS) Germany, translated by Zheng Yongyan.
3. Hirai Norio et al.: *The Last Words of a Nuclear Power Plant Employee.*
4. Ditto.
5. "The World Nuclear Waste Report 2019", Heinrich Böll Stiftung (HBS) Germany, translated by Zheng Yongyan.
6. Chen Hongmei: *Japan 3.11 Apocalypse.*
7. Reference: "Major Nuclear Accidents in History", "Fukushima Ten Year After" Lau Kin Chi et al., SDX Joint Publishing Company, 2021 Beijing.
8. Chen Hungmei: *Japan 3.11 Apocalypse.*
9. "The World Nuclear Waste Report 2019".
10. Clayton Crockett, Jeffrey W. Robbins: Religion, Politics, and the Earth.
11. Ditto.
12. Chang Yuchieh "Fukushima Daiichi Nuclear Power Plant Accident Handling Costs", Japanese News Translation Platform.

13. "10 Lessons from Fukushima—Reducing risks and protecting communities from nuclear disasters", Fukushima Booklet Committee.
14. Zhou Qi, executive director of National Institute of strategic studies, Tsinghua University "Is Tokyo Electric Power Company simply a business?", *Guancha*, March 29, 2013.
15. Re-starting Nuclear Power Completely—the Concern Left Behind by Shinzo Abe's Unexpected Resignation.
16. See Appendix in this book.

9

The Long Road Home

After the nuclear disaster, the Japanese government gave out evacuation instructions. When the evacuees left their homes hurriedly and in agitation, they thought they would be coming back soon. Among the various local governments in the neighborhood of the nuclear power plant, only a small number of them received the evacuation orders directly from the central government. Some of them had found out about the evacuation order only through television news and made the decision to evacuate the residents before receiving official notifications from their superiors. Most of the residents left without having received adequate information, and some did not even know that there had been a nuclear disaster emergency. The relevant central government departments repeatedly announced on television that the situation was not severe, that the evacuation notice was merely a precautionary measure. As such, many residents thought they could return home soon, and did not bring with them identification documents or items of significance. Even more sadly, they left behind their livestock and pets to their tragic fate, not realizing that they would be unable to return for a long, long period.[1]

K. C. Lau et al., *The Fukushima Catastrophe*, Global University for Sustainability Book Series, https://doi.org/10.1007/978-981-99-1956-7_9

A classroom at an evacuated elementary school in Futaba, April 2018. (Photo by Aihara Hiroko)

In an evacuated junior high school in Futaba, a clock and a radiation monitor are now placed on the school campus, April 2018. (Photo by Aihara Hiroko)

The evacuation process was hardly as smooth as that portrayed in the film *Fukushima 50*. When the earthquake occurred, some residents were not able to leave immediately because of insufficient fuel supply. They lined up in long queues at petrol stations waiting for refueling. Further, there were serious congestions on the roads between the coastal areas of Fukushima and the mainland. With the situation unfolding, the government's evacuation orders had extended from a radius of 2 km initially to 10 km, then 20 km. Did radioactive rays understand the numbers and stop along the 20 km radius? Of course not. Iitate village, about 30 km northwest of Fukushima Daiichi and a famous scenic area, was outside of the evacuation zone. Yet two months later the 1700 families there with 6200 people had realized they were subjected to radiation all that time, as the southeasterly wind at the time of the disaster had brought with it the radioactive substances.

On 14 March 2011, after a hydrogen explosion occurred at the nuclear power plant, a U.S. Army helicopter had found radioactive substance even 100 km from the plant, including Iodine 131 and Cesium 137. And on 16 March, the United States Atomic Energy Commission instructed all U.S. citizens within a radius of 80 km from Fukushima Daiichi to evacuate.[2] Yet the Japanese government had not further extended the 20 km evacuation zone for its citizens, but simply appealing to those in the 20 km to 30 km zone to stay home, with doors and windows closed 24 hours a day. Even then, 1.5 million out of the population of 2.3 million in Fukushima had to be evacuated. However, there were only enough shelters for 150,000. Many had to go to different places to find available shelter. Some became ill from exhaustion. The conditions in the shelters were quite harsh for mothers with children, the elderlies and the handicapped. They were over-crowded, with no air-conditioning in the onset of summer, temperature as high as 35 degrees Celsius. It was even more difficult for those from hospitals and nursing homes. Many could not endure the prolonged evacuation process and passed away.

The exclusion zone in Kawamata, Date County, Fukushima. Behind the "No Entry" sign and fence, the sun was shining, and no one was there. (Photo by Aihara Hiroko)

In areas 50 km away from the nuclear power plant, such as Koriyama, and Fukushima City where the prefecture government is located, there were no evacuation notifications. Many families with small children had left on their own due to health concerns, as radioactivity levels in the local water and soil were found to be higher than normal. They would not receive much compensation from TEPCO or support from the government, and have to bear the costs on their own. There were also many families where the father had stayed on to work while the mother took the children away. Such families had to bear the burden of doubled livelihood expenses. Quite a few couples, in face of the decision whether to evacuate, where to, until when, and so on, found that they could not agree. Some ended up separating and eventually divorced. That is how the term "atomic divorce" came about.

In Fukushima Prefecture and the neighboring areas, there had originally been many households with two, three generations. After the disaster, about half of the evacuated households had seen their family members dispersed.

Those who were not directly injured by the earthquake or tsunami but passed away later during evacuation due to indirect causes such as health deterioration, were referred to as "earthquake-related deaths". Of the three prefectures that were affected the most, Iwate Prefecture had 441 of these cases, Miyagi had 889 and Fukushima had 1704 (based on statistics as at end of March 2014). These included suicide cases in which victims took their own lives out of desperation, their homes having been contaminated and they felt there was no hope for the future.[3]

Minamisoma City, August 2012. Children are playing indoors to avoid radiation. (Photo by Aihara Hiroko)

What is even more horrifying, the impact of a nuclear disaster, unlike other natural disasters, is four-dimensional. Not only does it affect the entire area, but it will also stay in time for a long, long duration. The half-life of radioactive material could last several millenniums, and in some cases even tens of millenniums. For example, Cesium 239 has half-life of more than twenty thousand years. Even Marie Curie was not fully aware of the damage of radioactivity to the human body despite the many chronic diseases that she had contracted. Her manuscripts and notebooks are still radioactive today, and those who want to read them have to wear full protective gear. She had determined that the half-life of radioactive Radium is 1,600 years. That means it would be another 1,500 years before the radiation level of those manuscripts and notebooks would go down by half.

If you were one of the tens of thousands of people who had to evacuate, what would you bring when you leave home? Three months after the disaster, the evacuees were allowed to go back home for the first time to take their belongings. Yet since the radioactivity level was still very high, the occasion was limited to just two hours, and each person was allowed to fill only a bag of 75 sq. cm.[4] How cruel! What would you take? What could you retrieve from your home after it was destroyed by earthquake and tsunami, and been subjected to radiation for three months?

In a scene from the film *Homeland,* a very reasonable question was asked—why had those responsible for contaminating the land and killing the livestock not been arrested? The answer given by the police in the film was that there were no laws that would find them guilty. As such the only recourse for the victims was to accept reality and accept compensation. Yet what sums of money could buy one's homeland, one's treasured memories and healthy body, one's crops in the fields, and the animals that were slaughtered? Can there be price tags for all these? Still, a lot of people were indeed forced to accept reality.

Top: The mother with early symptoms of cognitive disorder cannot find her own shelter among the rows of identical grey resettlement houses, but she can clearly identify the way home in the forest without signs. Poster of the movie *Homeland* Bottom: The evacuation zone was empty, and the cows were starved to death. April 2011. (Photo by Toyoda Naomi)

If a nuclear war erupts and all humans and human-made artifacts wiped out, nature will probably still be there and will continue breathing. It will probably have sufficient patience to revive life on Earth over the course of hundreds of thousands of years, even millions or tens of millions of years. But it probably would not make the same mistake again of reviving the human species.

Notes

1. "10 Lessons from Fukushima—Reducing risks and protecting communities from nuclear disasters", Fukushima Booklet Committee.
2. "U.S.A. evacuating diplomats and military families in Japan", March 20, 2011.
3. "10 Lessons from Fukushima—Reducing risks and protecting communities from nuclear disasters", Fukushima Booklet Committee.
4. Chen Hungmei: *Japan 3.11 Apocalypse*.

10

Revival? Clearing Evacuees to Zero?

After the earthquake and nuclear disaster, the government had set the period for reconstruction to ten years, and established a temporary organization, the Reconstruction Agency, to handle this as well as the nuclear disaster aftermaths. On 2 March 2020, the Ministry of Agriculture, Forestry and Fisheries reported about the reconstruction. As at the end of January, reconstruction work in most disaster areas had essentially been completed, yet for Fukushima the proportion of completed reconstruction was only 71%. In view of this the Reconstruction Agency and its functions have been extended to March 2031.

According to reports by the Japanese media, out of 42 cities in the three affected prefectures, Iwate, Miyagi and Fukushima, 15 would not be able to complete reconstruction before 2020. Further, 11 of them indicated that it may not be completed even after 2021. What gave rise to this absurd situation was not merely the government's mismanagement. It was also related to corruption among officials in the disaster areas. The 6.5 trillion Yen disaster aid had not been fully used towards reconstruction. Large sums of money had simply disappeared.

K. C. Lau et al., *The Fukushima Catastrophe*, Global University for Sustainability Book Series, https://doi.org/10.1007/978-981-99-1956-7_10

In September 2013, Tokyo won the bid for the 2020 summer Olympics. To safeguard the construction of Olympics-related facilities, the government had reassigned many engineers and construction workers to Tokyo for the Olympics project. As a result, there were labor shortage in the disaster zones as well as rapid price inflation of construction materials. Undoubtedly, the Japanese government's move exacerbated the difficulty of reconstruction work. Yet Prime Minister Shinzo Abe had bragged that by 2020, the year of the Tokyo Olympics, the number of evacuees would be cleared to zero.

2020 has come and gone. Did the number of evacuees come down to zero? Let us take a look at the mental and material conditions of the common folks, aspects that the mainstream media have not paid much attention to.

In addition to a total of 22,000 for the number of direct and indirect fatalities as well as the number of those missing, there were more than 40,000 (as of March 2020, per Reconstruction Agency statistics) dispersed around Japan, not yet returned to their homes. Although by then only about 2.7% of the land in Fukushima was still restricted, being very close to the nuclear power plant, yet more than 60% of those interviewed indicated that they decided not to go back. In over one decade, many of those who left have already settled down in their new environment and do not have much desire to move again.

The Japan Broadcasting Corporation conducted a four-year tracking study on evacuated residents and found that 42% had decided not to return. Of these, 18% made that decision within one year of the disaster, 20% between one to two years, 25% between two to three years, and 33% made that decision in 2015, i.e., after four years. It shows that as time went by, they had less and less confidence in the reconstruction of their home village.[1]

The reconstruction and revitalization period set by the Japanese government has ended, yet it still seems a long way from real revitalization. Other than the slow progress of reconstruction work, problems of decontamination and secondary ecological hazards are still acute and hard to solve. However, to create the image that Fukushima is already 'revitalized' and normalized, the Japanese government has adopted many measures to drive the victims' return. Starting March 2017, no more housing subsidies were paid to those who evacuated on their own from outside of the designated evacuation zones. And except for 7 cities, towns and villages, in 2018 the government ended the work on decontamination.[2]

In many places the level of radiation is still very high and not suited for human habitation. The victims generally have the sense that the government is forcing them to return. Just a few days after the Fukushima disaster, on 14 March 2011, the government raised the acceptable radiation level on humans from 1 milliSievert (mSv) per year to 20 mSv per year. In comparison, after the Chernobyl disaster, the former Soviet Union had designated all areas with more than 5 mSv per year as mandatory evacuation zone.

Sievert is a measurement unit of radioactivity dosage. One Sievert equals 1000 mSv, and 1 mSv equals 1000 microSievert. The International Committee for Radioactivity Protection stipulates that the annual exposure limit for the public is 1 mSv, and many countries have adopted this standard. At the other end of the scale, a single dose of 7000 mSv would cause severe damage to the DNAs of an exposed body. There is no cure, and the person will die. At 4000 mSv, 50% of those exposed will find it fatal.[3]

The peculiarity and severity of radiation is that, unlike other substances, it cannot be diluted. Professor Tian Song vividly explained this. If the force of an arrow is divided into 10,000 parts by reducing its speed to 1/10000 of the original, then having it hit the body 10,000 times would not have caused the body any damage. That is the effect of dilution. However, if the force of the arrow is divided into 10,000 parts by splitting it into 10,000 small darts, then having them hit the body at the original speed of the arrow would cause the same damage as the arrow.[4] Nuclear radiation is like this; it cannot be diluted. Further, the effect will accumulate. It may not be noticeable in the short run, but over time, when symptoms of cancer such as leukemia emerge, it is too late. With regard to the research on radiation exposure effect, the survivors of Hiroshima and Nagasaki are being studied on the most. They were given checkups every year but not treatments. Anyone that do not arrive for checkups in a given year means probably that the person has passed away.

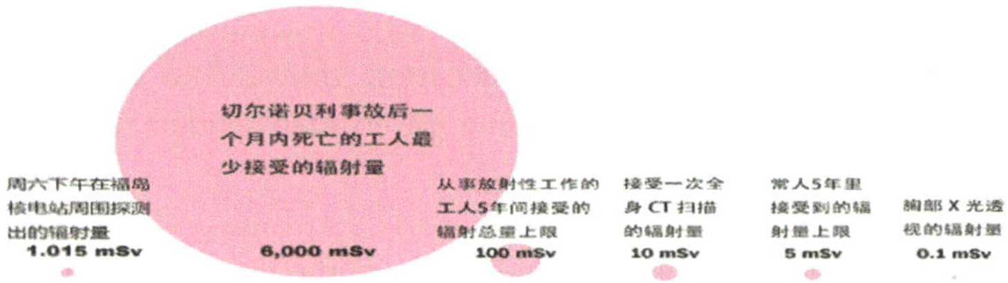

Radioactivity level detected around Fukushima Nuclear Power Plant the day after the accident 1.015 mSv	Radioactivity level that workers who died within one month of the Chernobyl accident had been exposed to 6000 mSv	Maximum radioactivity exposure that workers in radioactive-related field can accept in 5 years 100 mSv	Radioactivity level for one full body CT scan 10 mSv	Maximum radioactivity level that a common person can be exposed to in 5 years 5 mSv	Radioactivity level chest x-ray 0.1 mSv

The German government has recommended that Japan revised the acceptable exposure level back to 1 mSv per year. The Japanese government agreed to follow up, yet it has not implemented the revision.[5] Former UN Special Rapporteur on Human Rights and Toxics, Baskut Tuncak, expressed discomfort with the Japanese government's stance, and disappointed that Japan had not done anything to restore the acceptable exposure level to the previous standard.[6] The Japanese government has designated areas with radioactivity level of over 5.2 mSv to be "radiation management zones", but at the same time has encouraged people to live a "normal" life in those areas. The law stipulates that there cannot be activities for children in areas where radiation level is more than 0.6 micro-Sievert per hour, yet the nuclear safety standard for playgrounds has now been set at 6 times of that.[7]

In July 2015, Fukushima evacuees, victims and supporters organized a demonstration to protest against the revocation of the evacuation area (Photo by Aihara Hiroko)

To create an image of being back to normal, the government has strongly pushed for lifting accommodation restrictions in the contaminated areas around the Fukushima nuclear plant. That involves 55,000 residents. On 12 June 2016, the Fukushima prefecture lifted the order on a "restricted residence zone" for the first time, allowing evacuees to return. In March 2018, the government stopped evacuation subsidies. The evacuees were still worried about radioactivity and pointed out that the government was anxious to lift the restriction due to preparation for the Olympics. Those willing to return were mostly the elderly. Young couples with children did not want to return to a place still overshadowed by the nuclear disaster. They doubted the government's basis for lifting the orders.

In the town of Naraha, the restriction was completely lifted in September 2016, with the guarantee that those who came to live there would have a job as well as subsidies. Yet very few had taken it up.[8] In another case, in Tomioka of the Futaba District, a returning resident Ms. Nakayama found her happy anticipation of being back home dashed. Very few of those in her original social circle had come back. Further, the landmark that used to feature in the daily life of the residents—the old train station—had been replaced by a new one rather than being preserved, a decision made without consultation with the residents.[9]

The tsunami caused by the earthquake on 11 March 2011 had also given rise to the disaster at Fukushima No. II Nuclear Power Plant in Futaba District. The cooling function of the reactor had been lost at one point. Fortunately, it was able to complete a cold shutdown, and avoided the catastrophic situation as that in the Daiichi plant. In July 2019, TEPCO decided to decommission the 4 reactors at No. II Nuclear Power Plant.

In October 2018, a fence was erected in an area that was classified as "difficult to return" in Namie. One cannot go back home without the permission of the government (Photo by Aihara Hiroko)

The gate to the Namie town exclusion zone, 2018. Courtesy of Fukushima Beacon for Global Citizens Network (FUKUDEN) (Photo by Aihara Hiroko)

In another case, in Namie, Futaba, where the evacuation order had been lifted, the forest that was on the other side of the road from a kindergarten had radiation level as high as 1.8 micro-Sievert per hour. All 1584 measurement points in the forest had radiation level higher than the Japanese government's long-term target of 0.23 micro-Sievert per hour. Of these, 28 were higher than the recommended international upper limit for children, by 10 to 20 times.[10]

The Fukushima residents who evacuated to other places in Japan, regardless of whether they were from the disaster zones, have been subjected to unfair reception. For example, cars with Fukushima license plates were smeared with ridicule words, or they were refused service at fuel stations and parking lots. Fukushima students transferred to other schools were subjected to discrimination. Moreover, even among the evacuees there had existed a subtle sense of jealousy. That was the personal experience of Ms. Nakayama.

Evacuees from exclusion zones who could not return home have three choices: stay in evacuation shelters, stay with friends or relatives, or rent their own accommodation. The media often interviewed those who stayed in temporary abodes, yet that was only a small number, about 10%, Families with children were not accepted. Most people were like Nakayama, renting homes in non-exclusion zones in Fukushima—referred to as "in-prefecture evacuation". They would receive a subsidy on the rent. Then, the next biggest group, about 30%, were those who moved outside of Fukushima.

When Nakayama was evacuated, she could not stay in the shelter because of her pet. Fortunately, a relative was willing to let her family stay for a while. She recalled that since some evacuees had nowhere to go except the shelters, while others like her could stay with relatives, a sense of comparison had emerged among the different groups. The latter became subjects of envy. Yet as she described, staying with her relatives did not mean having a room with a bed to themselves. Her family were simply sleeping on the floor, on 'beds' that were made up of carton boards. Even those who stayed in shelters had this sense of comparison among themselves—which town were you from, was your town more / less affected by radiation? Everyone was a victim, yet the sense of envy arising from such comparison was prevalent.[11]

After the evacuees returned home they must still be vigilant, and they carry with them a radiometer all the time. Obviously, it does not feel good to be living fearfully in a completely transformed community. Those families with children have even more worries, the most direct being that regarding food. In Japan, most primary school pupils are given a nutrition lunch in schools, and the government has the policy of using local produce through local distribution. It is a policy that should have been applauded, yet in Fukushima it has added to the parents' worry.

Summarizing the reports from *Sankei Shimbun* (*Tokyo Daily*) and *Asahi Shimbun*, the percentage of Fukushima produce being used in nutrition lunch had dropped to just 18.3% at one point. Yet the report published in January 2019 showed that in 2018 it had risen to 40.8%, even higher than the percentage of 36.1% in 2010. The Fukushima Department of Education explained that it was due to the increased use of fruits and processed food produced in Fukushima. *Asahi Shimbun* pointed out that the Japanese government had encouraged local governments to increase the usage of local produce in nutrition lunch to over

30% by 2020. Further, Fukushima itself was giving special subsidies and incentives to raise the proportion of Fukushima produce being used.

On the one hand the government encouraged 'normalization' of Fukushima agriculture; on the other hand, the civil community was worried. Ms. Takahashi, who had no choice but to move back to Fukushima with her children because of her husband's job, was very cautious when shopping for food items. She would avoid Fukushima ingredients as much as possible. She would not have her child partake the nutrition lunch served in the school and would prepare a lunch box for him instead. Although there was no rule that all children must take the nutrition lunch, her child, being the only one who did not, had been looked askance at by other pupils. Finally, Ms. Takahashi was forced to transfer her child to another school where more children brought their own lunch. According to Ms. Takahashi, many parents were in fact worried about the safety of the children's food, yet not many would go as far as to have them bring their own lunch. Many made the excuse of "milk allergy" just so the child would at least not be drinking Fukushima milk while having the school lunch. In Ms. Takahashi's observation, the proportion of pupils certified to be "allergic to milk" has become very high.[12]

The mothers' worry is not without grounds. The municipal government of Nihommatsu, 35–70 kilometers from the nuclear power plant, had requested residents to send food samples for testing during the period from November 2011 to December 2017, whether self-grown, picked or purchased. The tests were for detection of Cesium 134 and 137. From these six years of testing, it was found that wild mushrooms exceeded the contamination limits the most. Next were wild vegetables. Other items were basically within government limits since 2015, but certain seed species such as chestnuts and ginkgo contained higher levels of radioactive substance after 2014.[13] One Japanese who was more than 70 years old told a reporter from *People's Daily online* that he would buy Fukushima agricultural produce in support of the reconstruction, yet he would not want his grandchildren's generation to consume them. He suggested that young people in general should not buy too much produce from Fukushima and the surrounding areas.[14]

There are many reasons for people to return home, yet only one reason for them to leave: the worry over radiation. That invisible menace has made it impossible for people to live there with peace of mind. Neither the government's guarantee nor the consolation money from TEPCO could comfort the people of that damaged land, people who paid a heavy price for the nuclear energy myth.

Notes

1. Chavin "Years after the Fukushima Nuclear Leak". https://zhuanlan.zhihu.com/p/20259639.
2. "99% of the contaminated soil to be reused?" cn.nikkei.com. https://cn.nikkei.com/politicsaeconomy/politicsasociety/35423-2019-05-06-05-01-00.html.
3. "10 Lessons from Fukushima—Reducing risks and protecting communities from nuclear disasters", Fukushima Booklet Committee.
4. Tian Song "Light of the Sun or Fire of Purgatory", see appendix in this book.
5. "Human Right Expert: Fukushima's nuclear radiation threat is still there; the government should stop work on moving back residents" United Nation News Network, October 25, 2018. https://news.un.org/zh/.
6. "United Nations Special Report on the Human Rights Impact of the Environmentally Sound Management and Disposal of Hazardous Substances and Wastes", October 25, 2018.
7. "Fukushima changed nuclear radiation acceptable safety standards for schools to be 20 times of that before the disaster". http://roll.sohu.com/20110525/n308431775.shtml.
8. Chang Yuchieh: "A brief overview of the current situation on the fifth anniversary of the lifting of the evacuation order in Naraha, Fukushima Prefecture" Japanese News Translation Platform. https://changyuchieh.com/2020/09/05/naraha/.
9. Chang Yuchieh: "Revisiting Fukushima II: Miss Nakayama from Tomiokacho Watch Shop", https://medium.com/kyosei-in-fukushima/nakayama-89bd02862603.
10. "Greenpeace says Japanese government misled UN over safety of children and decontamination workers", Greenpeace. https://www.huanbao-world.com/NGO/90216.html.

11. Chang Yuchieh: "Revisiting Fukushima II: Miss Nakayama from Tomiokacho Watch Shop", Japanese News Translation Platform. https://medium.com/kyosei-in-fukushima/nakayama-89bd02862603.
12. Chang Yuchieh: "Revisiting Fukushima III: Local Mothers' Worry – Is Fukushima still a place suitable for children's growth?" Japanese News Translation Platform. https://www.ncbi.nlm.nih.gov/pmc/articles/PMC6210092/.
13. Nobuaki Kunii, Maya Sophia Fujimura, Yukako Komasa, Akiko Kitamura, Hitoshi Sato, Toshihiro Takatsuji, Masamine Jimba, and Shinzo Kimura, "The Knowledge and Awareness for Radiocesium Food Monitoring after the Fukushima Daiichi Nuclear Accident in Nihonmatsu City, Fukushima Prefecture", *Int J Environ Res Public Health*, 2018 Oct; 15(10): 2289. https://www.ncbi.nlm.nih.gov/pmc/articles/PMC6210092/.
14. "The long road of rebuilding the disaster zone in Northeast Japan (the primary scene)" *People's Daily Online*, March 20, 2019.

11

Glint of Hope Ignited by the Olympic Torch?

The Japanese government meticulously and elaborately designed the campaign to promote the theme of "Fukushima revitalization" through the 2020 Tokyo Olympics, which was called "Olympics of Reconstruction". Likewise, the Olympics torch was named "the flame of revitalization". The Fukushima J-Village National Training Center was designated as the starting point of the torch relay. Built in 1997, J-Village was a sports training center about 20 kilometers south of Fukushima Daiichi Nuclear Power Plant. After the 3.11 disaster, it was used as the gathering base for personnel dealing with the nuclear dangers. Every day, thousands of people in full protective gear and carrying radiometers would be deployed from the training center to the power station. The J-village stadium was utilized as a helicopter pad, purifying center, temporary accommodation for personnel, as well as parking space for fire engines and armored vehicles. In the plan for the Olympics, J-village would be catching the eyes of people worldwide: when the Olympic flame arrived in Japan from Greece, the torch relay would set off from J-village, and after 121 days it would arrive at Tokyo's New National Stadium for the Olympics opening ceremony.

K. C. Lau et al., *The Fukushima Catastrophe*, Global University for Sustainability Book Series, https://doi.org/10.1007/978-981-99-1956-7_11

Other opportunities being planned for Fukushima included holding certain games like baseball and softball there to stimulate tourism, constructing Olympic gymnasiums with Fukushima wood, using food ingredients as well as hydrogen energy produced in Fukushima during the games, licensing Fukushima crafts as Olympic souvenirs, and so on. These arrangements seemed to have an effect distracting the public's attention. According to a survey in December 2019, 86% of the people believed that it was good to hold the Tokyo Olympics.[1] However, it was controversial internationally. The plan to supply meals prepared with Fukushima ingredients to athlete delegations worried the international society. The Japanese government declared that since 2015, Fukushima rice had not been found to exceed the radiation limit. Only freshwater fish and wild vegetables were found to be problematic.[2] Former prime minister Shinzo Abe claimed that he ate rice produced from the Fukushima disaster area every day. Yet that did not alleviate the public's concern. South Korea strongly requested the Japanese government to take responsibility and let the world know of any hidden radiation-related issues around the Tokyo Olympics. Further, Korea planned to have its delegation bring their own food and water. Greenpeace announced that in testing several spots close to J-Village on 26 October 2019, the radiation readings were found to be on the high side: ground level tests indicated a level of 71 microSievert per hour, which was 1775 times of that before the 3.11 disaster. The readings at 10 cm, 50 cm and 1 meter from the ground were 32, 6 and 1.7 microSievert per hour, respectively, compared to Japan's safety standard which is generally set at 0.23 microSievert per hour. Greenpeace believed that exposure to the detected levels of radiation would not be fatal if it was only for a short duration. Yet with the maximum acceptable annual exposure for the human body at 2000–3000 microSievert, that limit would be exceeded if one stayed around J-Village for just two days.[3]

Satirical posters on the Tokyo Olympics along the roads in South Korea

The Covid-19 pandemic that rapidly spread around the world changed many of these plans. Given that lockdowns and quarantine measures were being adopted worldwide in an attempt to contain the pandemic, and moreover all kinds of sports and public events were being cancelled, it was decided in March 2020 that the 2020 Tokyo Olympics would be postponed for a year. The International Olympics Committee and the Japanese government had tried very hard to avert this possibility, yet ultimately that 'difficult decision' had to be made.[4] According to estimates by the Xinhua News Agency, postponing the Olympics could possibly lead to a loss of US$ 3 million in commercial sponsorship and about US$ 12 billion in preparation costs for the games. It was the first time that the Olympics games had to be postponed in the 124 years of its modern history. The International Olympics Committee designated a maximum amount of US$ 650 million to pay for costs related to the postponement while the Tokyo Olympics Committee was still assessing the costs to be borne by Japan.[5] That US$ 650 million from the IOC might only cover a fraction of Japan's loss.

Japan insisted on keeping the label "2020 Tokyo Olympics" when held in 2021. In view of the pandemic, the Japanese people were not as enthusiastic about the games as before and turned more attention to averting the virus. In a survey conducted by the Japan Broadcasting Corporation in July 2020, only 26% felt that the Olympics should be held regardless, while some even appealed for its cancellation to redeploy the budget to Covid prevention.[6]

If the Olympics games were deemed a worldwide spectacular event that signifies world peace, friendship and solidarity, then radioactivity could be recognized as having an impact worldwide "equally" and without discrimination. No one can stay out of it. Fukushima might have already become a lone island on Earth, yet radiation from the nuclear disaster will continue to affect all life on earth for a long, long time to come.

Notes

1. "Huge preparatory investments and second wave of the Pandemic is underway: will the postponed Tokyo Olympics be held?" *The People's Daily Overseas Edition*, August 15, 2020, page 6. http://paper.people.com.cn/rmrbhwb/html/2020-08/15/content_2003482.htm.
2. "Have athletes sleep on carton mattress, eat Fukushima rice: the Tokyo Olympics created a legend of frugality" *China Business News*, November 27, 2019, https://www.yicai.com/news/100418111.html.
3. "Tokyo Olympics 2020: what is the economic impact of one year's delay?", BBC Chinese Website, https://www.bbc.com/zhongwen/simp/world-520.
4. "Tokyo Olympics delayed, the non-quantifiable economic account", Xinhua Net. http://www.xinhuanet.com/world/2020-05/24/c_1126025713.htm.
5. Chang Yuchieh: "After the Fukushima Daiichi Nuclear Power Plant accident, management personnel in Tokyo Electric Power Company were found not guilty in the judgement of first instance: a complete explanation on the first criminal case against a nuclear power plant", Japanese News translation platform.
6. Motoko Rich "6 years after the earthquake, the predicament of Fukushima's nuclear spent fuel is still insolvable" New York Times Chinese Network, March 13, 2017.

12

Where did Contaminated Substances Go?

On 19 September 2019, the trial concluded on three TEPCO senior management personnel, whether they had been negligent in causing the Fukushima Daiichi Nuclear Power Plant disaster. They were found not guilty. Before the trial concluded, TEPCO and the three defendants repeatedly apologized to the public and to the Fukushima residents. TEPCO indicated that the company would revitalize Fukushima, truly and sincerely undertaking damage reparation, decommissioning the reactors, decontaminating the area as well as strengthening the safety level of nuclear power plants; that TEPCO would not shirk its role and betray the public.[1] The question is whether TEPCO can honor its words.

After the disaster, everything in and around the site became radiation-contaminated substances that must be disposed of—the spent fuel rods and fuel debris from the meltdown reactors, building materials, debris from the nuclear power plant explosion, hundreds of tons of nuclear-contaminated water used in cooling down the reactors, contaminated soil and trees within a diameter of over 10 km, protective gears disposed

K. C. Lau et al., *The Fukushima Catastrophe*, Global University for Sustainability Book Series, https://doi.org/10.1007/978-981-99-1956-7_12

of by tens of thousands of decontamination workers, and so on. How to dispose of them, where?—the more deeply one thinks about these problems the more terrified one becomes. The disaster itself was only a starting point. Proper handling of the aftermath is the main part. However, the response that human beings are capable of is, as yet, crude and primitive. National borders cannot block radiation. It is not just a problem for Japan, but a burden that all lives on earth must bear together.

The Ministry of Economy and Industry stated that it would take half a century to completely decontaminate the site! By then, much of the dangerous radioactive materials would have started decaying. However, Japan does not have permanent storage facilities for the nuclear garbage, so it is still unclear where all of that would be stored. These are time-bombs that human beings have manufactured and buried, one after another.

Trees and Branches Cut from 89 Hectares of Forests[2]

There used to be wide spans of forests around the nuclear power station, part of which was designated as a reserve zone for birds. As the forests became contaminated by the nuclear explosion, workers had to cut down the trees within an area of 89 hectares. There had been a famous avenue of cherry blossoms in the neighborhood. The numerous cherry trees had to be cut down.

A radiation monitor in Fukushima Park, July 2015. (Photo by Aihara Hiroko)

Bulging garbage bags of contaminated substances against the background of rows of fruit-bearing persimmon trees in Namie Town, December 2018. (Photo by Aihara Hiroko)

3519 Containers of Radioactive Soil Used in Filtration[3]

The soil that was used in filtering the nuclear contaminated water also carried traces of radiation. As of March 2017, there were 3519 containers of varied sizes storing the contaminated soil. TEPCO indicated that the total quantity could not be ascertained, and the company was experimenting on ways to handle them. One way was to mix it with concrete or iron, and then decide on storage method later.

200,000 Cubic Meters of Radioactive Debris[4]

After the explosion during the reactor meltdown, the plant site was completely filled with debris from the fallen structures. Workers and robots were deployed to clear the ruins of concrete blocks, pipes and metal.

Based on TEPCO's estimation, as of 2017 the total quantity of debris cleared had exceeded 200,400 cubic meters, all radioactive. These were stored in specially made steel containers. The total volume was equivalent to more than 3000 standard 40-ft (12.2meters) long containers. Then there was also the earthquake debris. That was sent to places outside of the disaster area for storage, raising concern from residents in those places. Yet the public was not permitted to attend the closed-door discussion seminars convened by the Ministry of Environment. Even meeting minutes were not allowed public access.

In the two years starting from 2011, just the cost of handling earthquake debris had reached 1 trillion Yen.

Disposing of Protective Gear

Around 6000 workers would put on protective gear daily to work on clearing the site. They were recruited from out-sourcing companies. They were exposed to high risk, yet their pay was poor (this will be discussed in a later chapter). After each shift, their disposed protective clothing, masks, rubber gloves and shoe covers would be compressed and stored in steel cases piled up in the vicinity of the nuclear power station. Up to 2017, the total quantity had already reached 64,700 cubic meters.[5]

Given the enormous volume of radioactive garbage, the Japanese government decided to enlist help from all prefectures and send the garbage all around the country, to be burnt in incinerators there. The acceptable benchmark put forward by the government was that—after incineration, each kilogram of ashes would contain no more than 8000 Becquerel of radioactive substance. Yet there was no benchmark set for the incineration process itself, and that would have a direct impact on the atmosphere. It was indeed a plan for contaminating the whole country.

Sea of garbage bags (Photo by Polish reporter Arkadiusz Podniesinski in 2015)

6

14 Million Cubic Meters of Contaminated Soil

After the nuclear disaster, a large quantity of radioactive substances (Iodine 131, Cesium 134, Cesium 137 and so on) had been leaked to the atmosphere and was spread by the wind. When it rained these substances would fall on the soil and get absorbed, contaminating the soil. As such the first step in decontamination was to collect the contaminated soil. With what? Not some high-tech magical medium, but the plastic bags that we are all familiar with. These bags of radioactive debris were stored in temporary storage grounds designated by various cities, towns, and villages. The coordination process had not gone smoothly, and ultimately places like schools, parks, house gardens were designated.[7] Since 2015, bags of contaminated soil have been moved to intermediate storage grounds in Okuma and Futaba. By March 2019, these had already reached 2.35 million cubic meters, and estimated to reach 14 million cubic meters by 2021.[8] On the roads of Fukushima, one can often see green trucks filled with large garbage bags, starting points and destinations unknown—that information being classified.

In October 2019, Super Typhoon Hagibia brought torrents and floods to Japan. 2667 bags of radioactive garbage from a temporary storage ground in Miyakojima, Fukushima, weighing 1.3 ton each, were washed down into the Kodo River, a river that flows into the Pacific.[9]

According to the Japanese government, the plan was to store these in Fukushima "temporarily" until Cesium 137 (which has a half-life of 30 years) is reduced, after which they would be sent outside of the prefecture for ultimate handling. However, it has not been decided on where to or how. Given the sheer volume, it is too big a problem to handle at the present day, so leave it to time! The so-called decontamination process in progress now is no more than a matter of moving the contaminated material around.

A radiation monitor in Fukushima Park in July 2020. (Photo by Aihara Hiroko)

There were two proposals for recycling the nuclear contaminated soil. The first was put forward in June 2016, and it was to use the soil with Cesium radioactivity between 5000 to 8000 becquerel (Bq) per kilogram in infrastructure construction around the country. Because of opposition by the public, a second proposal was put forward in March 2017, which was to use the soil for landfill that will later be built up into parks. It was again met with strong protests. Relevant Japanese laws stipulate that radioactivity of reused material from dismantled nuclear plants should not be more than 100 Bq per kilogram. Both the 2016 and the 2017 proposals were well over this legal limit. Whether used in building infrastructures or green parks, the radioactive soil would be vulnerable to natural disasters such as floods and earthquakes, and potentially spread the radioactivity. It would take at least 170 years before the radioactivity level would come down to the legally stipulated safety threshold. In the meantime, nuclear contamination could also be spread around the country through underground water and through the air.[10]

Soil radiation meters were flashing, Minamisoma City, September 2017. (Photo by Aihara Hiroko)

Piles of garbage bags of contaminated substances, known as black pyramids, Naraha town, April 2018. (Photo by Aihara Hiroko)

Notes

1. Chang Yuchieh: "After the Fukushima Daiichi Nuclear Power Plant accident, management personnel in Tokyo Electric Power Company were found not guilty in the judgement of first instance: a complete explanation on the first criminal case against a nuclear power plant", Japanese News translation platform.
2. Motoko Rich "6 years after the earthquake, the predicament of Fukushima's nuclear spent fuel is still insolvable", *New York Times Chinese Network*, March 13, 2017.
3. Ditto.
4. Ditto.
5. Ditto.
6. https://www.podniesinski.pl/portal/fukushima/.
7. "Contaminated soil in Fukushima hard to dispose; the Japanese government declared that 99% of it can be reused" *Global Times*, February 26, 2019.
8. "Japan intends to reuse the contaminated soil in Fukushima", Nuclear and Radiation Safety Center of the Ministry of Ecological Environment, March 6, 2019.
9. Report by *Kyodo News Agency of Japan*, October 14, 2019.
10. "Fukushima contaminated soil to be used in building parks in green belt", https://news.ifeng.com/a/20170401/50874410_0.shtml.

13

Heart of Darkness—The Molten Reactor Core

On 16 December 2011, the Japanese government claimed that the damaged reactors at Fukushima Nuclear Power Plant had reached a stable state at a low temperature, and shamelessly announced that the "nuclear power plant incident has ended". Even disregarding the wide areas of exclusion zones that were still around the plant, it was clear what kind of a blatant lie it had been simply by observing the acute situation inside the plant. It was in 2012, after much procrastination, that TEPCO finally announced the scrapping of the cores of reactors 1 to 4 in Fukushima Daiichi Nuclear Power Plant.

The then Prime Minister Shinzo Abe visited the plant in December 2012. During the visit he said that closing down and dismantling the nuclear power plant would be an unprecedented challenge in human history. He did have that one right. Today, more than ten years after the accident, the situation was not much improved.

To dismantle the Fukushima Daiichi plant, which is like a time bomb, it is necessary to clear out the nuclear fuel, the nuclear waste and the radioactive substances that have continued to accumulate inside the

K. C. Lau et al., *The Fukushima Catastrophe*, Global University for Sustainability Book Series, https://doi.org/10.1007/978-981-99-1956-7_13

plant. The difficulty of that mission is hard to imagine. Even after ten years TEPCO is just beginning to scratch the surface.

There had been a long period of time during which little news on the decommissioning task was released because there was little progress due to the level of difficulty. At the same time, the public's attention had been diverted to the Olympics and the "revival" of Fukushima. The inside of the nuclear power plant was a darkness that the spotlights did not shine upon.

We waited until this point to take the readers inside the site for a look, not because it is not a key part of the disaster, but because it is too heavy a trip, so heavy that one would find it hard to breathe.

In February 2019, TEPCO and the Ministry of Economy and Industry held a joint press conference in Tokyo to present the status of scrapping the Fukushima Daiichi nuclear power plant. They indicated that reactors one to four had all been cooled to a stable condition. From Reactor Number 4, which was not in operation when the disaster happened, all 1,535 spent fuel rods were retrieved by the end of 2014. As for reactors 5 and 6, since their back-up power supply had not been destroyed, they suffered only minor damage and were already scrapped in January 2014. That was to say, reactors 4 to 6 were essentially dealt with. However, there were still more than 1600 fuel rods inside the spent fuel pools in reactors 1 to 3, where meltdown did occur.

The spent fuel rods emit very strong radiation. If they are not continuously cooled down, they would be melted by the high temperature. TEPCO was hoping that after cleaning enough of the radioactive debris, they could begin to handle the spent fuel rods. It is an extremely difficult task. Yet even more challenging is to clean up the fuel that had been in use inside the reactor cores when meltdown occurred. According to a study by The International Research Institute for Nuclear Decommissioning (IRID), a total of 257 tons of nuclear fuel had undergone the core meltdown. The molten fuel rods became mixed with other metallic material in the pressure vessel, and together the total weight was 880 tons.[1] That would be 6 times more than the debris taken out of the partially meltdown reactor core at Three Mile Island in the USA in 1979. Further, no one really knows what kind of conditions the highly radioactive debris was in, or their precise locations. According to plan, the vessels were to be completely sealed off and filled with water, and then robots would be deployed to search for the molten fuel fragments and clean them up. However, the ruins, with the contaminated debris, the fatal radiation level, and the risk of radiation leakage, have rendered the progress of this mission to a snail pace.

Let us take a look at what is known about each reactor's situation.

Reactor Number 1

Reactor Number 1 is still in the investigation stage. Inside, 392 fuel rods remained. Since there had been a hydrogen explosion at the time of the nuclear disaster, over 1,500 tons of construction material from the collapsed roof and building structures have scattered on top of and all around the spent fuel pool, hindering the progress of retrieving the spent fuel rods from the pool.

In 2017, TEPCO revised the progress chart and postponed the retrieval process. It was originally scheduled to begin in 2018, and the revised plan was to clear the debris by the end of 2021. After that, since the roof over the reactor had fallen off, it would be necessary to construct a large protective cover over it to prevent the spread of radioactive substances to the outside during the retrieval process. It follows that the retrieval process would only be able to begin in 2023.

In 2019, according to the report released on 20 December by Kyodo News Service, due to the many problems encountered, TEPCO and the Japanese government decided to further postpone the retrieval process by 5 years, meaning that it would only begin around 2028.[2]

As for the molten core, TEPCO had previously hazarded that most of the nuclear fuel inside had already pierced through the reactor's pressure vessel and fallen onto the safety shell, 'most likely' accumulating at its bottom. As to where, it could only be investigated by robots. An attempt to do so was made on 18 March 2017. At 30 cm and at 1 meter above the bottom of the safety shell, the radiation level in the contaminated water was 11 Sievert per hour and 6.3 Sievert per hour, respectively. The fact that the closer to the bottom the higher the radiation level did suggest the possibility of the molten fuel debris fallen to the bottom of the safety shell. Yet there was no mentioning of another more horrifying possibility, that the nuclear remnants had already pierced through the bottom of the safety shell.

Full completion of the scrapping mission is expected to take 30 to 40 years, which means it would only be completed by the 2040s to 2050s.[3]

Reactor Number 2

There were 615 fuel rods remaining in Reactor Number 2. It was at one time regarded as having the worst problem.

On 16 February 2017, a robot designed by Toshiba with camera lens at the front and back entered the safety shell of Reactor Number 2. It turned out that the radiation level was as high as 530 Sievert per hour, more than 7 times than earlier estimates. A person exposed to it would die within seconds. The robot was expected to work inside for over 10 hours, but with the high radiation level it lasted no more than two hours. As its mobility had been hindered by obstacles inside, it could not be retrieved and was left buried inside. The investigative probe was a failure. From images taken, TEPCO was able to partially ascertain the condition inside. For example, at the lower part of the pressure vessel an accumulation of molten fuel seemed to be there, also the support frame seemed to have partially fallen off. There were holes about 1 meter in length on the support frame, likely caused by the hot fallen fuel eroding and piercing through the pressure vessel and landing on the safety shell. No one knows whether the safety shell itself had been eroded and pierced through.

In February 2019, TEPCO announced a turning point in the investigation, and described in detail the probe that was conducted on 13 February from 7 am to 3 pm. During this operation, a remote-control device in the shape of two "fingers" was lowered by cable down to the bottom of the safety shell. It was able to touch the accumulated substances in 6 spots. For five of these, it was ascertained that the accumulated substances, several centimeters in size, were pebble-like in some and rod-shaped forms in others and were movable. Some could be lifted by as high as 5 centimeters. To some extent they were firm, not dilapidated or crooked.

TEPCO's public relations personnel indicated at the press conference that this probe had proved the possibility of retrieving the fuel fragments. As to other items that could not be grasped by the device, it would be necessary to perform more research and design usable devices. The press conference gave the impression that there was a breakthrough in the cleanup process, that the high-tech robot had been successful in completing the mission. Yet, on further thoughts, one wonders with the robot able to lift a pebble-like fragment by no more than 5 centimeters, what is to be done with the hundreds of tons of nuclear remnants that are inside this reactor? That is of course the next question to be asked, yet the spotlight had merely focused on the small robotic hero.

TEPCO said, before starting retrieval of the fuel rod remnants it would be necessary to first build a storage facility for them, and as such a preparation period would be needed. According to the plan announced by the government in December 2019, instead of initiating retrieval in 2023 as originally scheduled, it would be postponed by one to three years, to the 2024-2026 timeframe, for the start of the Herculean project.

Reactor Number 3

According to the Japan Broadcasting Corporation's report on 15 April 2019, the fuel rod retrieval process which would involve 566 fuel rods would be postponed by 4 years and 4 months. Postponement had happened time and again because the radiation level above the reactor had not come down to the expected level. Moreover, an additional protective covering over the building had to be constructed to prevent the spread of radioactive matters when the spent fuel rods were being retrieved. If everything goes smoothly, all of them including 52 unused ones would be retrieved by March 2021.

On 19 July 2017, TEPCO announced the investigation result of the first robotic probe inside Reactor Number 3. The robot weighing two kilos, measuring 30 centimeters long and 13 centimeters in diameter, was named "small sunfish". It had taken two days just to have it enter the reactor. Four teams of workers were involved, taking shifts to conduct the operation. Even in full protective gear, they could only stay inside the reactor building for several minutes at a time. On the second day after entering, the small sunfish recorded the first sign that the uranium fuel had melted inside the reactor. Underwater images taken showed that the reactor was badly damaged. However, the molten and fallen fuel had not been located.

According to the report by *Fukushima Minpo* on 2 December 2019, that day the government announced a plan that for the first time set an end date. The retrieval of fuel fragments from the reactor cores would start from 2021, to be completed by 2031. Reactor Number 4 was already cleaned up, but reactors 1 to 3 still had 4741 portions of nuclear fuel remnants. After these are taken out, they would be put into water tanks in other buildings inside the nuclear power plant. However, such tanks at present can only take up 666 portions of remnants.

Some people are of the opinion that it would not be possible to safely clean up the radioactive material, and suggest leaving them there, building a 'cement tomb' over it with concrete and steel, similar to that at Chernobyl. Yet, given that to date it has not been possible to find out precisely the conditions inside the reactors and the whereabouts of the molten nuclear fuel, and further, given that the molten nuclear fuel have not completely cooled down, it would not be feasible to seal it with concrete like the Chernobyl case.

It was estimated that by 2030, the contaminated solid waste and the nuclear remnants inside the reactors would weigh a total of 770,000 tons. The government said that by 2028 a plan would be designed to categorize, decontaminate, and store these materials.[4]

Rian Whitton, an analyst of ABI Research Institute, expressed that the Fukushima disaster was an "embarrassing moment", that "it showed the limitation of robotic technology at the present."[5] As described earlier, the robot in Reactor Number 2 had successfully lifted a pebble-sized fragment to a height of 5 cm. Yet how many tons of nuclear remnants are there in the 3 reactors altogether? The answer is: around 250 tons, and what is more, extremely radioactive with positions unknown. If one were to timidly whisper the question, "then how many robots, working for how long, would be required to retrieve all of that, and where would that be stored?", these questions would be treated as inopportune. The Japanese government and TEPCO have no answer.

It looks like even the best scientists in the world have no answer. Lake Barrett, senior adviser for TEPCO, said it was equivalent to sending someone to the moon. Barrett was responsible for the cleanup at Three Mile Island. Despite this scientifically advanced age, in which artificial intelligence seems ready to take over human labor, the disaster at Fukushima has shown human beings to be at a total loss about what to do. Taking one step at a time on the chess board, they fake moving forward. They are placing bets on our global ecology and human survival. One wrong move and all is doomed.

Notes

1. "Other than the nuclear contaminated water, Japan is also facing a challenge that is unprecedented in human history…." Outlook Think Tank Observer stationed in Tokyo, November 2, 2020.
2. "To prevent radioactive material from scattering, the Fukushima Nuclear Power Plant postponed retrieval of fuel rods from two reactors", https://baijiahao.baidu.com/s?id=1653573397773351647&wfr=spider&for=pc.
3. "Delayed by more than 4 years, today Japan begins to retrieve nuclear fuel rods from Fukushima's Number 3 reactor", https://www.guancha.cn/internation/2019_04_15_497695.shtml.
4. "Japan revises Fukushima cleanup plan, delays key steps", December 27, 2019. https://apnews.com/article/d1b8322355f3f31109dd925900dff200.
5. Roger Cheng: "For Fukushima's nuclear disaster, robots offer a sliver of hope", CNET, March 9, 2019.

14

Returning to the Scene: "Back Then, How Nice It Would Have Been, If Only …"

If only the embankment were constructed to be 15 meters high as originally proposed! If only Reactor Number 1 had been timely decommissioned! If only seawater were immediately used to cool down the reactor core! If only all that were true there would not have been the astronomical cleanup cost and compensation cost of today, there would not have been tens of thousands of people still unable to return home, there would not have been the problems of disposing radiation contaminated material and dealing with its impact on lives and the ecology. Yet why had these thoughts not come to mind and the actions not taken back then?

Japan Broadcasting Corporation (JBC) interviewed more than 100 of those who were on site at the time directing and working, and collected a large amount of firsthand information, trying to clarify as much as possible what really happened.[1] Through these interviews, they found that those in charge of rescuing the situation had pinned their entire hope on the "self-initiating emergency cooling mechanism"—not something particularly advanced or novel, just a cooling system to be used in

K. C. Lau et al., *The Fukushima Catastrophe*, Global University for Sustainability Book Series, https://doi.org/10.1007/978-981-99-1956-7_14

case of accidents that all nuclear reactors have. Under normal circumstances, if all external power sources are lost, the cooling process would self-initiate. However, the water capacity it has is quite limited and can only last for a short time. It would be necessary to initiate a diesel power generator to supply power for cooling, until such time as normal power supply is resumed, or until the reactor core is cooled to a stop. Unfortunately for Fukushima, the functionality of the diesel power generator had been destroyed by the tsunami. Even if the self-initiated cooling mechanism had worked, it would only delay the meltdown, and could not preserve the reactor.

At the time, those on site were in fact not even aware of the most basic operational design of the emergency cooling unit - that when power supply stopped the cooling unit would shut down. As such, in the event of an emergency, they must have someone manually turn open the unit's valve to initiate it. Yet they simply assumed that the unit would come into operation by itself. JBC reviewed the records taken at the time and there was nothing said about checking the status of the cooling unit after the power supply stopped.[2] The investigation report also noted that the personnel operating Reactor Number 1 were not sufficiently trained on operating the cooling unit, and that was very improper for a nuclear power plant.

Those in charge had also referred to another juncture that might have helped the situation but lost due to wrong judgment. When the central control room regained partial power supply with the tsunami's retreat, the staff immediately turned on the cooling unit to inject water into the reactor core. The water instantly evaporated, and the steam they saw led them to believe that the reactor was in a safe state. The steam went quickly, indicating that the cooling water had dried up. To avoid overheating the waterless cooling unit, they decided to shut it down. That decision was made on their assumption that the reactor was still in a safe state, which turned out not to be the case.

While they had admitted to this kind of wrong judgment that led to wrong decisions, they avoided discussions on the most critical problem—not maintaining the cooling process by using seawater. It would have been the most effective and direct approach, yet because of self-interest,

TEPCO had kept procrastinating on it. If this approach were immediately undertaken to cool the three reactors, the temperature inside would have been reduced sooner, and meltdown could have been averted. In that case the explosion might not have happened, and the radioactive substances would not have leaked. A major environmental catastrophe would have been avoided. As it was the key decision that had led to the catastrophe, it should have been the basis for determining responsibility on what had happened. As such they had avoided talking about it, trying to distract domestic and international public attention away from it.

After the hydrogen explosion in Reactor Number 1 the working team began injecting seawater to cool it down, which was effective. Anyone would think a similar approach would immediately have been undertaken for Reactors Number 2 and 3, yet it was not. TEPCO was still hoping for miracles. Then Reactor Number 3 had an explosion and after that they started to inject seawater to it, but still not Reactor Number 2 until even the latter's protective shell had exploded. It could be surmised from this sequence of events that the working team was not deciding on those actions haphazardly while in panic. They appeared to have a clear goal, to execute senior management's priority of safeguarding the reactors' operational functionality by avoiding the use of seawater. So long as there was no indication of a meltdown, they would not give them up, meaning that they would not change the approach.

As a matter of fact, back in the 1970s the Fukushima nuclear disaster had already been 'previewed' in court. When the Ikata Nuclear Power Plant in Ehime was built, the local residents had opposed it strongly, but they were ignored. In 1973 the residents brought a lawsuit against the local government, demanding a statement on the probability of the worst-case scenario—core meltdown. The case went from the local court to the Supreme Court and lasted 19 years. The plaintiff lost. Looking back at the court arguments of this case, every critical element that the government claimed could not possibly happen had indeed occurred in the Fukushima disaster: power outage—heated nuclear fuel rod—water injection—meltdown—leakage.[3] Every statement of "it won't happen" or "it is impossible" turns out to have been false reassurance. Back then, how nice it would have been if only.

Notes

1. "Japanese media replays the whole course of the Fukushima Nuclear Power Plant accident: two opportunities wasted", https://news.qq.com/a/20120310/000096.htm?emfhe4.
2. Li Yuan, Wang Xuan "Lies and Arrogance: The Truth of Nuclear Disasters in Japan".
3. Ditto.

15
Absent Supervision

In July 2007, a 6.8 Richter scale earthquake struck the Kashiwazaki-Kariwa Nuclear Power Plant, in the vicinity of Niigata. The plant was designed to withstand an earthquake of up to 6.5 Richter scale. One of the reactors had been struck by a force more than 2.5 times of its anti-seismic capability. Fortunately, all four reactors at the plant had closed down automatically and there was no leakage of radioactive substances.

Soon after that, in August 2007, a famous Japanese strategist referred to this incident in his book and considered it an extremely fortunate eventuality. He suggested that a safety check on nuclear power plants be conducted as soon as possible but was not taken seriously by the Japanese government. On the contrary, that extremely fortunate eventuality had reassured Japan and reinforced the myth around nuclear safety. Even those who made up the myth started believing in it.[1]

In fact, ever since the first nuclear power plant started operation in Japan in July 1966, there have been all kinds of accidents. The underlying reason is the loophole in supervision that makes it possible for the nuclear energy industry to fake safety reports, hide fatal accidents, understate the risk level of earthquakes, and so on. The Fukushima catastrophe

K. C. Lau et al., *The Fukushima Catastrophe*, Global University for Sustainability Book Series, https://doi.org/10.1007/978-981-99-1956-7_15

was predictable, if not inevitable, the outcome of an encounter between natural disaster and human-caused calamity.

Fukushima Daiichi nuclear plant had a total of 6 reactors, the biggest nuclear power station in the world. An emergency response center had been built especially for the Fukushima plant. Yet its design was only sufficient to withstand a Richter scale 7 earthquake. Internal documents in TEPCO showed that the company had never conducted tests against scale 9 earthquakes. The cliff along the coast of Fukushima is 35 meters high. If the power plant were built on top of the cliff, it would have escaped the 15-meter tsunami. Yet the design, brought in from the U.S., would not fit a site at an altitude of 35 meters, and to have it changed by the U.S. would have been quite costly. As such TEPCO decided to cut corners by leveling the cliff down to 10 meters to suit the U.S. design.[2]

In the 1960s, Japan had strongly promoted nuclear power and had gobbled up the atomic power generation technology of the U.S. A "turn-key" agreement was reached in 1966 with General Electric (GE), in which GE would completely handle the design and manufacturing of the entire operation, and Japan simply had to 'turn the key' to initiate it. That was how the Fukushima nuclear power plant was constructed. At the time, Japan believed everything would be fine given that the technology was from the United States. No one had thought of the risk of having the emergency power generator installed underground. It was not just one person who failed to think that through for Japan, but everyone involved.[3]

Another reason for the disaster was aging of the equipment. Usually, the life cycle of a nuclear power plant is 40 years. The Fukushima power plant was built in 1971 and was ready for decommissioning. On 7 February, just a month before the earthquake, TEPCO issued an analysis report on the Fukushima nuclear reactors, pointing out various issues around aging of the equipment. Yet, neither TEPCO nor the Japanese government took it seriously. In celebrating the 40th anniversary of the Fukushima power plant, TEPCO made the wild claim that the life cycle of nuclear power plants could be extended to 60 years, and The Nuclear and Industrial Safety Agency (NISA) agreed. As such, decommissioning was postponed to 2031.

Whether the risks of earthquakes or aging of equipment—these are solvable problems. Yet why were they not handled on a timely basis? The fundamental reason is the flaw in the supervision over nuclear power, appearing most blatantly as politician-government-finance collaboration, the media's collective misrepresentation, and the industry's "self-regulatory" model.

When the major accident occurred in Fukushima, the Inspector General in charge of the plant had only found out from the news a day later. Those at the scene of emergency could hardly be blamed for not having had the time to make a report. As such the authorities are always shut out from those kinds of situations.[4] Even Naoto Kan, the then prime minister, only found out about the explosion in Fukushima through television news reporting. It was like what Chief Editor Yoichi Funabashi of *Asahi Shimbun* had said, "Japan's nuclear safety supervision system is in name only. The supervisors pretend to be supervising and the nuclear power companies pretend to be under supervision."

The Fukushima disaster exposes the supervision flaws in the system.

First, supervision lacks autonomy. The NISA comes under the Ministry of Economy and Industry while the Nuclear Safety Commission comes under the cabinet. Both are government administrative organizations. Personnel movements happen frequently between NISA and the Agency for Natural Resource and Energy, the institution responsible for leading nuclear power development, thus largely compromising safety supervision. NISA has been caught in a scandal of 'manipulating public opinion'. One nuclear power plant operator had admitted that NISA suggested inviting nuclear power supporters to join policy discussions so as to 'balance' the voice on the anti-nuclear side. In late 2013, the Japanese Parliament passed the Designated Secrets Protection Law, under which nuclear-related information can be concealed in the name of "national safety" and "designated secret".

Second, effective supervision over nuclear power companies is lacking. Nine legally related issues have been pointed out by the Japanese scholar, Yoshihiro Nishiwaki: factors for nuclear plant installation permits are unclear, the standard for installation permits is not explicit, approval basis for a project is biased towards structural specifications and does not include quality assurance, functional and performance specifications are too simplistic, the relationship between installation permit inspections and project plan approval inspections is unclear, safety regulations are entirely related to operational management and there is confusion between basic design requirements and operational management requirements, the structure adopted of control by phase lacks restraining power, there are too many safety inspections and too much duplication that prevent flexible checks, and there are no real checks on the processing of fuel substances.

In 2007, TEPCO publicly admitted that since 1977, among the 199 scheduled inspections on its three nuclear power plants, there had been major negligence as well as manipulation of data and covering up of safety hazards.

Takashi Hirose, a free-lance media practitioner in Japan, has published an article in *Diamond* magazine after the Fukushima disaster, entitled "Could the Collapse have been avoided? Facts behind the Fukushima Nuclear Power Plant". In it, he severely criticized the collusion of politicians, government, and financial groups around nuclear power, pointing out that during the Liberal Democratic Party administrations, the whole series of nuclear power polices had been influenced by the Federation of Electric Power Companies of Japan as well as the Japan Business Federation. Among those in-charge in these organizations, many had come from the electric power industry.[5]

The Ministry of Economy on the one hand has pushed strongly for development of the nuclear power industry and on the other hand has performed the key role in nuclear safety inspection. With this kind of flawed system, it is not surprising that the nuclear safety department has not performed effective supervision on nuclear facilities, hence the frequent accidents.

After the Fukushima disaster, people worldwide have not seen much reflection and self-reproach among the Japanese nuclear power sector. On the contrary, the latter has been covering up the truth, diverting pertinent discussions, and adopting delay tactics to wear down people's patience and attention. What they probably hoped for was to keep the incident low-profiled so as to muddle through.

In December 2018, a Japanese brewery in Namie Town was left in a state of disrepair after the earthquake and nuclear accident. Since the evacuation, no one has ever come back, and time seems to have frozen. (Photo by Aihara Hiroko)

Notes

1. Li Yuan, Wang Xuan "Lies and Arrogance: The Truth of Nuclear Disasters in Japan".
2. Ditto.
3. Ditto.
4. Hirai Norio et al.: *The Last Words of a Nuclear Power Plant Employee.*
5. "Southern Energy Watch: The Japanese Nuclear Apocalypse", April 26, 2011. https://news.qq.com/a/20110426/000530.htm.

16

Radioactive Contamination Spread Worldwide—The Threat from Nuclear-Contaminated Water

In October 2020, the Japanese government intended to approve the plan to discharge into the ocean 1.23 million tonnes of nuclear contaminated water that has been stored at the Fukushima Nuclear Power plant. This once again caused uproars domestically and internationally. The "Fukushima nuclear catastrophe" once again appeared on the front pages of international news.

Water is the beginning of life. No one can survive a day without drinking and using water. It is the most precious gift from Nature that we rely on for existence. What we did not anticipate was that the monstrous nuclear power plants' survival also depended on water, and in huge quantities. Whether in operation or decommissioned, nuclear power plants need to use enormous quantities of fresh water to cool down the nuclear fuel. Even nuclear power plants in normal operation would continuously release nuclear-contaminated water to the ocean, every hour, every moment. Although there are restrictions on the volume being discharged as well as the concentration of radioactive substances in it, this still results in contamination of the water body.

K. C. Lau et al., *The Fukushima Catastrophe*, Global University for Sustainability Book Series, https://doi.org/10.1007/978-981-99-1956-7_16

After the Fukushima nuclear catastrophe, water was injected into the nuclear power plant for cooling, generating huge volumes of radiation-contaminated water. On another front, because the western part of the plant is on a higher altitude, around 200 tonnes of underground water flows every day from west to east where the nuclear reactor is, thus becoming contaminated.

TEPCO has tried many ways to reduce the volume of contaminated water. One might be in awe upon hearing about the advanced technologies being deployed. To block the underground water that continued seeping into the reactor, in 2017 the government spent 35 billion Yen to build an underground frozen soil wall (ice wall) surrounding Reactors Number 1 to 4. Yet it had a one-percent leakage, and TEPCO reported on 1 March 2018 that the wall could only reduce the volume of contaminated water by 80 tonnes daily. Therefore, other methods such as drop shafts, Advanced Liquid Processing System (ALPS) and so on were undertaken as supplements. With these, the average daily volume of contaminated water being generated was reduced from 540 tonnes in 2014 to currently 110 tonnes.

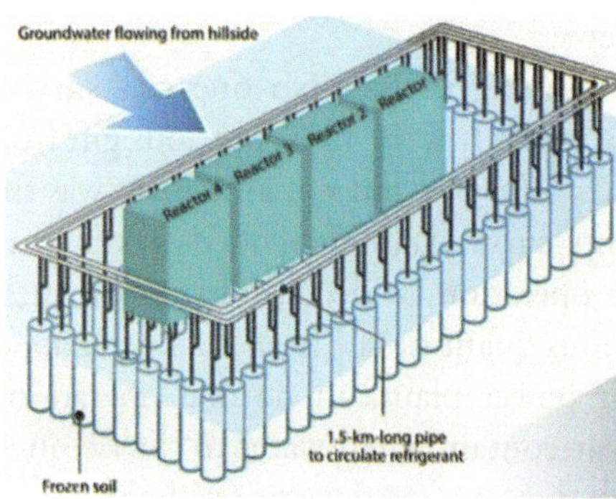

Design of the frozen soil wall around the 4 reactors, 1.5 km in length, 30 meters underground

Soon after the nuclear accident, in April 2011, TEPCO had already discharged into the ocean low-level radioactive contaminated water that were stored in Fukushima Daiichi power plant before the accident. The explanation was that there was no time to build temporary storage tanks for the high-radioactive water, and as such, it was necessary to empty out the 11,500 tonnes low-level radioactive water that was there to make room. Yet even this so-called 'low-level radiation' exceeded the legal permissible concentration for discharging by 100 times.

This irresponsible action gave rise to strong resentment from the fishery industry in Japan and from many other countries. The German marine research institution, Geomar Helmholtz-Zentrum, did a simulation in 2012 to estimate the spread of Fukushima nuclear contamination in the ocean, and the results indicated that within 57 days, radioactivity had spread to more than half of the Pacific Ocean. It would only take three years for the contamination to reach Canada and the United States.

Under pressure from strongly adverse public opinion, TEPCO was forced to stop discharging the water and ultimately built large tanks for storing the water.

At present, the contaminated water is being stored in more than 1000 grey, blue and white tanks. As of September 2020, TEPCO had built 1044 storage tanks on the plant site, and the volume of stored contaminated water reached 1.23 million cubic meters. The building of water tanks would stop at the end of 2020, when the total capacity would be up to 1.37 million cubic meters. According to a Jiji News Agency report, in a government committee meeting convened in August 2019, TEPCO had projected that the contaminated water with radioactive substances would completely fill the storage tanks by 2022.

What is to be done after that? TEPCO put forward five proposals: increase the capacity and the number of tanks, set up other sites for storage tanks, solidify the water and discharge it into the ground then release it into the ocean after processing, and lastly, discharge it into the atmosphere in the form of steam. Eventually, it came down to two proposals, discharging into the ocean or into the atmosphere.

The approach of discharging the water into the ocean is envisaged as follows: process the contaminated water to reduce the concentration of radioactive nuclear elements to the permissible level except for Tritium, then dilute it with large quantity of uncontaminated water to reduce the Tritium concentration to 1500 Bq per liter. Yet the dilution would hugely increase the volume of water to be discharged, estimated at around 700 million tonnes. It would prolong the time needed for the discharging process to 30 years.

TEPCO does not like to use the term 'nuclear contaminated water' and refers to it as 'processed water' after it has gone through the Multi-nuclide Removal Equipment (APLS) purifying mechanism. Greenpeace denounced this terminology as misleading to the public, giving the wrong impression that it is clean, with Tritium as the only residue element. In fact, that is not the case. According to Shaun Burnie, nuclear expert from Greenpeace's German office, even after processing, the contaminated water still has other radioactive elements such as Iodine-129, Strontium-90 and Ruthenium-106. Some of them are the worst radioactive elements, and fatal if the concentration is high.

A report released on 18 February 2020 by Kyodo News Agency indicated that residue substances were found repeatedly in the storage tanks of processed water. The public criticized TEPCO for not proactively disclosing such findings, and not being transparent about their handling of the residues. TEPCO merely expressed that in future if residues were found in other storage tanks, then there would perhaps be a need to further investigate and to conduct more purification processes before releasing the water into the ocean.

The proposal to discharge contaminated water into the atmosphere is similar in most respects, heating and evaporating the processed water that has Tritium concentrations at less than 5 Bq per square cubic meter, then discharging it for it to be blown away by the wind. Obviously, this approach is not as convenient as releasing into the ocean. Further, it has the effect of causing the fear that people might be breathing radioactive air. As such the proposal that TEPCO focused on was discharge into the ocean. The plan was repeatedly leaked to the public to test their acceptance. Although strong opposition was raised every time, after the many attempts people appeared to have grown accustomed to the idea.[1]

A demonstration was held in Fukushima against the discharge of nuclear wastewater from the Fukushima Daiichi nuclear power plant into the ocean. (Photo by Aihara Hiroko)

Such approaches of using quick and cheap short-term solutions, without regard to potentially perilous long-term consequences, are precisely the kind of choices that greedy, selfish and short-sighted capitalism is most adept at making. The acting chairperson of the Japanese citizen group "Atomic Force Citizens Committee" and the director of the international environmental protection organization FoE Japan, Ms. Kanna Mitsuta, put it frankly to the reporter from *The Paper*, "after the nuclear plant accident, Fukushima fishermen have been working very hard to try and revive the fishery industry. Yet the government and TEPCO have attempted repeatedly to convince them to accept the plan of discharging contaminated water into the ocean, not giving any regard to the reasons against it that the fishermen raised."[2]

What is the impact of that radioactively contaminated water on the environment and the human body?

In August 2020, the U.S. journal *Science* published a report stating that the Fukushima nuclear contaminated water contained many radioactive substances. Among them was tritium in high concentration, very difficult to remove. Another substance was Carbon-14. It would be easily absorbed by marine organisms and could accumulate to a concentration that is 50,000 times of tritium. These are potentially toxic to humans. Further, the half-life of Carbon-14 is very long at 5370 years. *Science* pointed out that once the nuclear contaminated water had been discharged into the ocean, it would cause serious contamination to the marine environment. The radioactive substances could spread to the entire Pacific region, perhaps even the entire global marine environment.[3]

Greenpeace also opposed this kind of method. They released a report on 23 October 2020, pointing out that the contaminated water would cause damage to human DNA.

A survey conducted by Japanese news *Yomiuri Shimbun* showed that 50% of the Japanese people disagreed with the proposal to discharge contaminated water into the ocean. The local environmentalists and fishery industry representatives were particularly adamant in their opposition. The Atomic Force Citizens Committee released an open statement on 20 October 2020, protesting the approach. Their statement pointed out that the contaminated water would contain many radioactive substances aside from Tritium. Although TEPCO indicated that they would perform a second 'processing', one would not know what the result of this second processing was, what radioactive substances might remain, and how damaging they would be to the human body. The statement said that while the issue of the contaminated water had been a subject of public concern ever since the accident in 2011, yet the Japanese government and TEPCO had not until then been able to propose effective measures to deal with it. The problem has been dragged on.[4] The fishery industry representatives told Kyodo News Service their worry, that once the contaminated water was discharged into the ocean, rendering some fish unable to meet the safety standard, it would be a disastrous blow to the entire industry.[5]

Radiation measurement by Mothers' Radiation Lab Fukushima (TARACHINE) of seawater near Fukushima Daiichi Nuclear Power Plant, June 2020. (Photo by Aihara Hiroko)

Former Japanese Prime Minister Yukio Hatoyama posted an article on social media criticizing the Japanese government's plan and indicated that the government should listen more to the voice of private industries. The Fukushima Reconstruction Common Center, made up of various organizations including the Fukushima Prefectural Committee of the Japanese Communist Party, submitted an appeal letter to the Minister of Economy, Trade and Industry, firmly opposing the discharge of nuclear contaminated water into the ocean, and stressing that it should continue to be stored on land.

The Japanese media pointed out that contrary to TEPCO's claim that there was no land available to build storage tanks, there were in fact large areas of uninhabitable land in the vicinity of the Fukushima Daiichi Power Plant given the high radioactivity level there. These tracts of lands can be used to build new storage facilities. The Atomic Force Citizens Committee believes that using large storage tanks on land or solidifying it with mortar are the best ways under existing technology.[6] Not long after the nuclear accident in 2011, Professor Koide had suggested storing the contaminated water in Japan's 100,000-tonne oil tankers.[7] Unfortunately, the Japanese government simply let the problem drag on, and the original 100,000 tonnes of contaminated water have become almost a million tonnes now, making it increasingly difficult to manage.

Regardless of the devout pledge from the Japanese government and TEPCO that the discharged water would meet accepted standards, there are still reasons to worry. Standards are set by people, and people do not know enough about the impact of radioactivity on marine organisms. Discharging the contaminated water into the water body—which occupies 70% of the globe—simply on the claim that it would not harm the human body is a totally irresponsible and selfish approach. Further, in the management of accident aftermaths, TEPCO has been found with repeated cases of violating rules, not reporting or even lying about problems, and so on. In 2015, the Company had given a written commitment to Japan Fisheries Association that "it would not take the approach of discharging into the ocean lightly".[8] Yet it is precisely doing so now, seemingly with full justification.

In an interview with *China Daily*, Lu Yaodong, Director of the Diplomatic Research Office of the Institute of Japan under the Chinese Academy of Social Sciences, said, "If Japan on the one hand represents itself as a major force in environmental protection, but on the other hand intends to discharge nuclear contaminated water into the ocean, it would do damage to Japan's international image. In this regard, Japan should give priority to the consideration of global environmental protection, not just be concerned with its own national interest."

On the other side of the Sea of Japan, Korea has been paying close attention to this issue of disposing of nuclear contaminated substances ever since the accident. At the sixty-fourth General Conference of the International Atomic Energy Agency, Korea's first official of the Ministry of Science, Technology, Information and Communications, Jung Byung-sun, expressed concern over Japan's intention of discharging the Fukushima nuclear contaminated water into the ocean, and stressed that Japan should communicate to the international society with transparency. Jung indicated that discharging contaminated water would impact the entire global marine ecology. There should be full assessment of the feasibility of this approach as well as its damage in the intermediate and long term, also closer cooperation with concerned nations and the international society. Before deciding on the plan, Japan has the obligation to conduct transparent communication with the international society, including Korea, in accordance with international laws such as the United Nations Convention on the Law of the Sea, so that the international society would have a full understanding and would be able to accept the related risks."[9]

The *Korea Times*, in relation to the proposal of discharging contaminated water into the ocean, criticized the Japanese government with the heading "cheap but dangerous", indicating that it would be a disaster, damaging the marine ecological environment system. It pointed out that Tritium would lead to cellular damage and mutation, eventually resulting in cancer, if accumulated in the human body over an extended period.[10]

Because of the effect of ocean currents, the radioactive substances would spread to the entire Pacific Ocean, and even further to the entire global marine environment. As such it is not solely an issue just for Japan, but an international issue that concerns the global marine ecology and environmental security. In June 2020, United Nations Human Right experts openly appealed to Japan not to neglect their human rights obligation with regard to disposing of nuclear waste, and expressed the hope that Japan would delay the decision until adequate international discussions could take place after Covid-19. The experts indicated that the disposal of nuclear wastes would have a profound effect for many generations to come. It would be a human rights issue that concerned not only Japan but also people outside Japan.[11]

There are at present 455 nuclear reactors in operation around the world, scattered over 32 countries and regions (up to November 2020 per International Atomic Energy Association). If Japan is allowed to set a precedent with discharges from Fukushima, it is not hard to imagine other nuclear power plants following suit to reduce costs, discharging so-called low-level radioactive water into the ocean.

In the context of this global threat, it is foolhardy selfishness for one to be concerned only with the safety of seafood and vegetables imported from Japan. The issue is more like the opening part of a doomsday story in science fictions: ignorant human beings discharging large volume of radiation contaminated water into the ocean, resulting in DNA mutation in various species of marine organisms, gradually affecting the entire food chain, which then comes back to haunt human beings... We are no strangers to such a plot in films, literature, or games. Yet, when it shows up in the real world, why are we so numb and blind, so indifferent and disinterested?

Notes

1. Sagittarius A "million tons of Fukushima contaminated water to be released into the Pacific, can we still enjoy seafood happily?" Guoke Net, http://www.world-ecological.com/news/1474.html.
2. Kanna Mitsuta, "Is there no other way but to release the contaminated water from the Fukushima Daiichi nuclear power plant into the ocean?", https://imidas.jp/jijikaitai/a-40-139-20-03-g707.
3. "If the million tonnes of Fukushima nuclear contaminated water is released into the ocean, it would pollute the environment and damage human DNA", October 27, 2020. https://world.gmw.cn/2020-10/27/content_34311356.htm.
4. "Japan's plan to release Fukushima's nuclear contaminated water raises concern", *People's Daily*, October 23, 2020.
5. "If the million tons of Fukushima nuclear contaminated water is released into the ocean, it would pollute the environment and damage human DNA", October 27, 2020. https://world.gmw.cn/2020-10/27/content_34311356.htm.
6. "Japan's plan to release Fukushima's nuclear contaminated water raises concern" *People's Daily*, October 23, 2020.
7. Hiroaki Koide exclusive interview, Radio Hong Kong, May 4, 2012.
8. "Japan's plan to release Fukushima's nuclear contaminated water raises concern", *People's Daily*, October 23, 2020.
9. Ditto.
10. "If the million tons of Fukushima nuclear contaminated water is released into the ocean, it would pollute the environment and damage human DNA", October 27, 2020. https://world.gmw.cn/2020-10/27/content_34311356.htm.
11. "Concern raised by Japan's plan to release Fukushima's contaminated water into the ocean" BBC Chinese website, October 26, 2020. https://www.bbc.com/zhongwen/trad/world-54675012.

17

Who Protects Decontamination Workers and Nuclear Energy Workers?

Decontamination work is in principle the responsibility of governments at all levels. In practice it is mostly outsourced to large construction companies and the civil engineering industry. It was hoped that these contracts would serve to stimulate local reconstruction. Yet most of the contractors are companies outside of Fukushima. Only low-level subcontracting was given to local small and medium sized companies. Moreover, on-site workers who directly handled the tasks have been recruited from all over the country.

This kind of multi-level contracting is not unique to decontamination projects, but a long-established structure widely found in Japan's civil engineering industry. With commissions deducted at every contracting level, the remunerations being paid to low level workers are far from commensurate with the importance or the risk-level of their work. On the other hand, companies that were profiting from nuclear energy development all along again have opportunities to gain from clean-up projects after the accident.

Take the case of truck drivers who transport contaminated soil. They work 8 hours a day with no lunch breaks because there is nowhere to

K. C. Lau et al., *The Fukushima Catastrophe*, Global University for Sustainability Book Series, https://doi.org/10.1007/978-981-99-1956-7_17

stop for lunch. Why do they come to work in Fukushima? "We see signs along the road regarding radioactivity levels, and we also carry radiation detection meters, yet radiation is not visible. So far, our bodies have not experienced anything unusual, so we are not too concerned about radiation."[1]

On-site cleanup work had started with 3000 people in 2013 and increased to a peak of 8000. Because of shortages of supply as well as inadequate government oversight, some contracted Japanese companies have in recent years turned their avaricious minds to overseas labor, refugees and the homeless. Some of them were cheated into going to Fukushima to handle the work that most Japanese are unwilling to do. As of 2016, official numbers indicated that around 77,000 people had been employed in decontamination work. Among them, some were eager to rebuild their home villages, some were local young people with few employment options, but more were underprivileged groups and homeless people. With the need to safeguard their livelihood, they would not say anything even in face of exploitation.[2]

United Nations human right experts Baskut Tunjak, Denius Plath, and Urmira Bra issued a joint statement in Geneva on 16 August 2018, appealing for concern over the conditions of Fukushima "decontamination" workers. The statement indicated that those employed in decontamination tasks included foreign workers, applicants for refugee status, and homeless people. The possibility that these people might have been cheated and exploited was worrying. They were compelled by financial difficulties to accept the risk of radiation exposure, and furthermore they did not have adequate training nor protection facilities.

In July 2018, Japan's Ministry of Justice published a survey, showing that of the four construction companies that have employed foreign workers for decontamination work, one had arbitrarily held back the special daily subsidy from the government to each worker, giving out less than a third of the subsidy to workers.[3] On the books, the daily pay for decontamination workers was 17,000 Yen, yet that did not mean the workers were well-paid. Cases of unpaid overtime hours and weekends, arbitrary holdbacks for room and board, and so on, were rampant. Some contracting companies were alleged to have even faked health certifications that they forced the workers to sign, or faked employees' identities, making it hard for the government to perform oversight.[4]

In those poor working conditions, the laborers would accumulate doses of radioactivity in their bodies, increasing the risk of cancer. Many workers who became experienced had to resign as they also became sick. Many of those employed by sub-contractors were not in a union or covered by medical insurance. When they got sick or injured, the sub-contractors usually would not allow them to apply for workers' compensation, the reason being that it would make trouble for upstream contractors. As a result, hidden cases of work-related injuries were widespread. It was back in 1975 that Japan had the first case of paying compensation on radiation-induced illness, but it was not affirmed as due to occupational injuries. Up until 2013, only 16 cases had been affirmed as such.[5]

Shaun Burnie, senior nuclear expert at Greenpeace's Office in Germany, quoted in a 2019 report a statement made by United Nations Human Rights Special Rapporteurs in August 2018 to the Japanese government, "we are deeply concerned about possible exploitation by deception regarding the risks of exposure to radiation, possible coercion into accepting hazardous working conditions because of economic hardships, and the adequacy of training and protective measures."[6]

That report was released on 8 March 2019 by the Japan Office of Greenpeace, titled "On the Frontline of the Fukushima Nuclear Accident: Workers and Children". It revealed that the Japanese government had deliberately misled international human rights organizations and experts, with cases including violation of agreements on labor rights and children's rights. In the report, a former decontamination worker, Mr. Minoru Ikeda, told of the inhuman treatment he had suffered. He indicated that some people even compared the decontamination workers to slaves. He wanted to disclose his personal experience to the public to appeal for Japanese government's respect for labor rights, stop sending people to such high-risk jobs, and moreover, provide appropriate support to the workers.

While we criticize TEPCO on the plight of decontamination workers, we should not neglect the fact that low-level workers in nuclear power plants are also an exploited group and are the most vulnerable when nuclear power plant accidents occur.

Before the Fukushima accident, there was little reporting by the media on the issue of nuclear energy plant workers' exposure to radioactivity. Although there has been some support from non-government groups, on-site workers have been muted about the conditions they experience due to the control that energy companies have on information. Generally speaking, the lower the subcontracting level, the higher the radioactivity exposure to their workers—97% of the radioactivity dosage has concentrated on these workers. From the time of the accident to March 2014, there were 174 workers with cumulative radioactivity dosage over 100 Millisievert, some as high as 678 Millisievert. The standards set for exposure are not only for safeguarding of health, but also applicable to identification of occupational disaster and insurance claims. On 16 March 2011, just a few days after the accident, the Japanese Ministry of Health, Labor, and Welfare changed the legal limits for acceptable radioactivity exposure from 100 to 250 Millisievert. Those who had exposure higher than 100 Millisievert in a year were given no more than an annual cancer checkup.

Another aspect is, to control exposure dosage the working hours for nuclear power plant workers are shorter than "regular" jobs. In high radioactivity areas, the actual working time for a day may only be 10 or 20 minutes. As such, workers do not have much of a sense of the risk of radioactivity exposure even if they are aware of the possibility of future problems. That makes it all the more important to manage radioactivity exposure strictly. However, according to Japan News Network, as early as 18 March 2011, highly radioactive substances had already been detected in Reactor Number 3. By 24 March, that was also the case for Reactor Number 1. Yet TEPCO had not communicated the information to the on-site workers. On 25 March, Nuclear and Industrial Safety Agency of Japan indicated that 17 workers had been exposed to radioactivity of more than 100 Millisievert.

When the accident happened, many of those who remained on-site to deal with it were prepared for self-sacrifice. Generally, the latent period for heavy radioactivity exposure is 20 to 30 years. That is what prompted the creation of the Fukushima "senior death squads". TEPCO requested old, retired volunteers to handle the deadly situation, not because they were more experienced or skilled, or that their lives were not valuable, but because even if they were exposed to high doses, they probably would not live to the time when cancer is expected to occur. In July 2011, a squad comprised of more than 400 retired nuclear energy experts and technicians was set up. The leader, 72-year-old Yasuteru Yamada, declared that being advanced in age, they would have no concern about radioactivity exposure and were ready to sacrifice their lives to deal with the nuclear leakage. Less than 3 years after taking up the assignment, and having entered the danger zone many times, he passed away in 2014 from cancer induced by high doses of radiation he had been exposed to—unfortunately not able to survive the supposed 20-year latent period that was promised.

The film *Fukushima 50* was based on the story of 69 workers who remained in their positions at the time of the accident. Every one of them had had exposure of 100–250 Millisievert, about 5 times the legal limit for nuclear power plant workers in the United States. Director Yoshida who demonstrated his bravery during the disaster also suffered from cancer soon after due to the high radioactivity level he was exposed to, and passed away in 2013 at the age of 58. It was not until 2018 that Japan first acknowledged any case of death due to radiation exposure. This was a 50 + male worker who worked on Fukushima power plant's nuclear leakage cleanup, and passed away due to radiation-induced lung cancer.

It is not only in nuclear power plant accident cleanup tasks that workers in the nuclear energy industry would be vulnerable to high degrees of risk. They are equally vulnerable in normal operation, and not adequately covered by medical protection. Their plights have been there all along, but not publicized due to information suppression by vested interest groups. It is only after accidents happen that the suffering of these peripheral groups is revealed. In 1979, Kunio Horie wrote the book *Nuclear Gypsy—Records of Exposed Subcontracted Workers*. It became a bestseller after the Fukushima accident with four reprints. To learn about the life of these people, he had taken up employment at a nuclear power plant. In the book he wrote, "Hearing it a hundred times is not as good as seeing it once. Every day is filled with surprises. Can there really be this kind of inhuman working environment in this world?"

Masao Hirai was a top level TEPCO technician who turned around to join the anti-nuclear movement. He passed away in 1997 because of cancer. He had talked of an incident that happened: one time a screw became loosened in the reactor that was running. The radioactivity level being emitted was very high. To fasten the screw, 30 people were made to stand in a row 7 meters from the screw. Each person, on hearing the order of "get set, run" would take turns to run up and try to fasten it. Each person could only stay to the count of three, at which point the alarm would sound. Some of them could not even manage to find the wrench before the alarm would sound. In this way, just wrenching the screw for three turns had cost 4 million Yen's worth of manpower. It may seem strange that the plant would not stop operation then do the repair work. That was because stopping operation for a day would cost up to 100 million Yen. In the eyes of the company, money is more important than human lives.[7]

On 4 August 2011, the Japan Bar Association Headquarters for Poverty Countermeasures published their findings. It revealed the dark secrets of this industry through the stories of three nuclear power plant workers. The Association concluded that they were Japan's lowest level laborers. After multi-tier subcontracting, the compensation that would have befitted the high-risk, high-contamination work was substantially reduced. The workers were mostly employed on short-term temporary basis. They did not have social security and were subject to dismissal at any time.

In the film *Pandora*, the main character who fortuitously became the hero was one such unwilling worker at a nuclear power plant. He would have preferred to leave home for two years to do hard labor on an ocean fishing boat rather than to work at the plant. Yet in his small town there was little choice. His father and brother had both worked in the plant and died in an accident. In real life, just as in the film, nuclear power plants are mostly built in remote rural areas—land is cheap, and it is easier to 'manage' when something happens. Those who come to work at the power plants probably do not do so out of love for the work. They are forced by poverty into making the hard choice of health or income.

Notes

1. Chang Yuchieh "Entering Fukushima Daiichi Nuclear Power Plant (II)" Diary on Collection of Material on Fukushima, https://medium.com/kyosei-in-fukushima/fukushima-driver-103cecf03c9f.
2. Greenpeace "Eight years after the Nuclear Disaster, Fukushima decontamination workers are covered in Blood and Sweat". https://www.greenpeace.org/taiwan/update/1530/核災八年，福島除污工人血汗蒙塵.
3. "United Nation experts warns Japan, decontamination workers are being exploited" Xinhua Net, August 18, 2018, http://big5.xinhuanet.com/gate/big5/m.xinhuanet.com/world/2018-08/18/c_129935033.htm.
4. Greenpeace "Eight years after the Nuclear Disaster, Fukushima decontamination workers are covered in Blood and Sweat". https://www.greenpeace.org/taiwan/update/1530/核災八年，福島除污工人血汗蒙塵.
5. "10 Lessons from Fukushima—Reducing risks and protecting communities from nuclear disasters", Fukushima Booklet Committee.
6. "Greenpeace says Japanese government misled UN over safety of children and decontamination workers", https://www.huanbao-world.com/NGO/90216.html.
7. Ditto.
8. Hirai Norio et al.: *The Last Words of a Nuclear Power Plant Employee.*

18

Mourning of Nature

After the Fukushima nuclear accident, residents within 20 kilometers of the nuclear power plant were urgently evacuated. In the rush, people were not able to attend to their animals, be it cats or dogs or cows. After the region was designated a restricted zone, residents were not able to return. Hence, there were ghastly cases such as an entire herd of dairy cattle tied up inside a barn starved to death.

K. C. Lau et al., *The Fukushima Catastrophe*,
Global University for Sustainability Book Series,
https://doi.org/10.1007/978-981-99-1956-7_18

Dead ostriches on a farm. The ostriches were starved to death after the humans left (Photo by Ohashi Masaaki)

The cows wandered around because their owners had released them. Later, the cows were captured and slaughtered (Photo by Ohashi Masaaki)

The town Tomioka in Fukushima Prefecture is 12 kilometers away from Fukushima Daiichi Nuclear Power Plant. All residents had been evacuated except Naoto Matsumura, who insisted on staying to take care of his own animals as well as those abandoned in the neighborhood.

In June 2011, a photographer Yasusuke Ota went to the area within 20 kilometers of the power plant to feed the abandoned animals. He met

Naoto Matsumura during his stay. While taking care of the stray animals, the photographer took pictures of them. In 2011 he published a book entitled *The Abandoned Animals of Fukushima*, in 2012 *The Fukushima Animals Continue to Wait*, and in 2015 *Shiro, Sabi, and Matsumura* that recorded the daily lives of Naoto Matsumura living with stray cats.[1]

Likewise, Masami Yoshinori from the town Namie in Futaba Prefecture took the risk of returning to the area to look after her 360 cows, the herd that she could hardly bear to abandon. After the nuclear accident, strange white spots had appeared on the bodies of the cows. She believed it was because they had been feeding on radiation-contaminated pasture, which caused gene mutation. What had upset her was that, after reporting it to the government, there had not been any assistance given. They came to take some blood samples and were not heard of again.

Photo by Motoki Noike

Photo provided by Hasegawa Kenji

The anthropocentric perspective would probably be concerned only with self-preservation, such as whether vegetables and seafood from the disaster region were fit for consumption. However, it was humans who caused the disaster. They only have themselves to blame for the consequences. On the other hand, the animals, birds, plants, and marine organisms that were also adversely affected did nothing wrong. Their health was impaired, their habitat was contaminated – who would compensate them, apologize to them, look after them? The mistakes made by humans had to be paid for by the lives of other species.

In Fukushima, as contamination of the forests has not been cleaned up, the animals that inhabit the area have been badly hurt. Anders Moller, an ecologist from the National Scientific Research Center of France, and Timothy Mousseau from the University of South Carolina, have performed statistical research on 57 species of birds from 400 areas at various levels of contamination. Their records show that in the more seriously contaminated areas, the number and the diversity of birds were sharply reduced. Mousseau said that their team had performed research in Chernobyl where the ecological environment was similar, and the findings there might be applied to explain the reasons for this. Many of the birds there had contracted cataracts and cancer, the size of their brains had shrunk, their fertility was weakened (especially male birds). These factors have weakened the survival ability of the birds.

Researcher Chiyo Nohara from the University of Ryukyus, driven by a sense of responsibility to posterity, overcame numerous difficulties and went to Fukushima two months after the accident, to study radiation-induced mutation on Oxalis Butterfly, a common species of butterfly found in Fukushima. His research found that the wings of the male butterflies had become smaller, their offspring had genetic abnormality, some of them had three antennae, their movements were sluggish, and their death rate was higher than that in other regions.[2] Other researchers have found that in the seriously contaminated areas, most of the fir trees have growth abnormalities. Furthermore, budworms in the proximity of the nuclear power plant were found to have deformities, while rice seedlings there were found to have activated the DNA repair mechanism to deal with radioactivity. Other than these fragments of findings, there have not been any overall assessment on mutation of the land ecological system as impacted by high radioactivity.

Research by Fukushima University in 2016 found that inside the evacuation zones, wild boars that carry radioactivity have multiplied rapidly, from 3,000 in 2011 to 13,000 in 2016. These wild boars cannot be used as food. Their bodies were piled up in large numbers after being hunted.

Wild animals like racoons also increased substantially in number, to the extent of three or four times the previous levels. Since the residents have moved away indefinitely, wild animals find it easier to roam about looking for food. Kei Okuda, Specially Appointed Assistant Professor, who conducted the research, pointed out that not only would they affect the lives of residents when the latter were able to return, they would even hinder their return. As to what kind of health issues might emerge when wild animals have been exposed to overdoses of radioactivity, there is next to no research data.

Another research team from Fukushima University, after a study conducted over 6 years, found that radiation levels in river trout around the nuclear power plant were six times the acceptable threshold. Radioactive substances that leaked into the rivers have followed the food chain and entered the bodies of fish. In Maedagawa town, which is 15 kilometers away from the power plant, various species of fish were also found to be well above the legal limits for radiation levels. That means the ecology of Maedagawa is already noticeably contaminated.

In addition to directly impacting animals and plants on land, and in water close to the site of the accident, radioactive substances have also entered and affected the global marine ecology through contaminated soil, underground water, as well as contaminated water discharged into the ocean.

In 2011, Nicholas Fisher from Stony Brook University found that, at a distance of 600 kilometers from the Japanese coastline, plankton and small fish in the ocean generally carried radioactive cesium. Another research in 2011 revealed that along coastlines within 30 kilometers of Fukushima, there were no longer any traces of rock shell conch.

The Oceanology Research Institute in Germany published a report in the March 2013 issue of the authoritative journal *Environmental Research*, pointing out that there had been at least 500 tonnes of contaminated water being discharged into the ocean daily. More than half of the area in the Northern Pacific had been found to have radioactive substances in the water. In Autumn of 2013, radioactive contamination would have spread to Hawaii and in 2015 to the Pacific Ocean west of the United States. The seawater in the Pacific would fall into a state of decay, with more than half of the organisms dying over the next 20 years. Regrettably, this projection is gradually being proven to be correct. On 27 March 2019, researchers from the University of Alaska had found higher than normal levels of radioactive Cesium-137 in the water sample close to St. Lawrence Island in the Bering Strait.[3]

While in the Pacific the concentration of cesium would have been diluted to a level below the legal limit, yet in the water within several kilometers from Fukushima, the cesium concentration remains higher than it was before the accident. Another substance that calls for attention is radioactive strontium. The concentration of strontium in seawater close to the nuclear power plant has not come down. This may be due to repeated cases of leakage from the storage tanks. The effect of cesium on the bodies of living organisms is similar to that of potassium. It will be absorbed and will circulate fast. And strontium is like calcium, it would accumulate in bones. These radioactive elements hence would exist in some of the fish for a long time.

It is noteworthy that there is very little research on how the Fukushima accident impacts the marine ecology system, even though the resulting volume of radioactive substances being discharged into the ocean is unprecedented. The few studies that have been done could not raise sufficient attention. People still know very little about the effects of the accident on marine organisms.

In 1953, United States President Dwight Eisenhower put forward the slogan "Atoms for Peace". Almost 70 years have gone by. That nuclear experiment, with the global ecosphere as gambling chips, has failed time and again. The shambles created by the hands of ignorant and arrogant people are unmanageable. During this course, humankind seems to have forgotten that when Nature nurtures life, it is to have life enriched and diversified through cycles of life and death, to become increasingly beautiful in the long process of evolution. Whereas, modern civilization, lost in the pursuit of short-term profits, continues to invest in the manufacturing of monsters. As one saying goes, "There are mistakes in Life; humanity is the biggest mistake of Life."

Notes

1. OTA Yasusuke's website: https://ameblo.jp/uchino-toramaru/.
2. "The 'butterfly effect' of the nuclear accident in Fukushima, Japan", Swiss Information, swissinfo.com.
3. "First time contaminated substances from Fukushima nuclear disaster found in Barling Sea" Xinhua net, March 29, 2019. http://www.xinhuanet.com/world/2019-03/29/c_1210094415.htm.

19

From Nuclear Weapon to Nuclear Energy, From Nuclear Energy to Nuclear Weapon

Japan's nuclear energy generation capacity is next only to that of the United States and France and ranks third among nuclear power countries in the world. Although the government continues to promote that Japan has a demand for nuclear power, after the 11 March 2011 nuclear disaster, with 54 nuclear power plants all suspended, the supply of electricity has been able to meet Japan's energy demands. As such we want to ask the question, given that a nuclear reactor is like a risky bomb, particularly when Japan is situated on a seismic belt, why does it want to drive nuclear power development so adamantly?

No one would be naïve enough to believe that nuclear power development is simply for the sake of electricity generation. Nuclear energy technologies derive directly from nuclear weapons developments carried out during the Second World War. Former Prime Minister Naoto Kan, after his retirement, said in a public speech in September 2013 that the development of nuclear energy around the world was not for electricity generation to start with. The motive of every country was to extract plutonium to make atomic bombs. The half-life of plutonium is very long at about 24,000 years.[1] The wishful thinking that this is a story of

K. C. Lau et al., *The Fukushima Catastrophe*, Global University for Sustainability Book Series, https://doi.org/10.1007/978-981-99-1956-7_19

redeploying the military industry to peaceful technological development, a story of turning the ferocious to being compassionate, is irredeemable ignorance.

Regarding the right to "peaceful" use of nuclear power, Japan's situation is rather unique. Of all the non-nuclear-weapon states that signed the Treaty on the Non-Proliferation of Nuclear Weapons (NPT), Japan is the only one that has commercial-scale reprocessing capabilities. The total stock of plutonium in Japan accounted for 1/5 of the 230 tons of civilian-use plutonium around the world. Since 2010, the United States repeatedly requested Japan to return the plutonium that it had provided to Japan during the Cold War. The bulk of that is weapon usable, and in theory can be used to make 40 to 50 nuclear weapons. Japan refused the request time and again, with the reason that the plutonium was needed for research and development of fast neutron reactor.[2]

The historical paradox is that, both the restriction and the re-initiation of Japan's nuclear power research have much to do with the United States. In 1945, after the defeat of Japan, the U.S.-led United Nations completely forbade Japan to develop nuclear-related projects. Seven years later, the U.S. manipulated 49 countries into signing the San Francisco Peace Treaty with Japan. It was a mal formation that still impacts Asian politics today. After it came into effect on 28 April 1952, all nuclear-related projects became permissible in Japan.

The reason that the United States changed its stance to support nuclear energy industries in certain countries has much to do with the Cold War context then. On 29 August 1949, the Soviet Union successfully carried out its first atomic bomb test blast, challenging the U.S.A.'s nuclear monopoly status. In December 1953, U.S. President Dwight Eisenhower presented his speech "Atoms for Peace" at the United Nations, clearly indicating that the United States would not object to "peaceful uses" of nuclear energy. However, the premise for the proposal was that those countries that engaged in nuclear energy development would not develop nuclear weapons. Eisenhower hoped to block other major powers from nuclear-related development unless they submit themselves to international regulations and inspections. In exchange for agreeing to the peaceful use of atomic energy, the United States would provide nuclear facilities, fuel and technology to these countries. In the

1960s, the U.S. began to support India's nuclear energy development in order to counter the socialist countries, that is, the former Soviet Union and China.[3] The so-called 'Atoms for Peace' proposal was permeated with the smell of blood right from the start.

In March 1954, parliamentary members from the Japan Improvement Party, including Nakasone Yasuhiro, Saito Kenzo, Kawasaki Hidey and Inaba Osamu, submitted a budget proposal of 235 million Yen to the Parliament, based on the name of the element "uranium 235", for the research and development of nuclear power. The bomb that was dropped on Hiroshima in 1945 was precisely a uranium 235 atomic bomb manufactured by Dupont. That irony of history set off Japan's nuclear energy industry on its way.

This unexpected budget proposal had shocked many scholars in the Japan Academic Council. Yet their plea was rejected by members of parliament. Nakasone Yasuhiro even said with disdain, "these bookworms would not come round unless one is to throw tons of money in their face."

Japan's attitude towards nuclear power has been dubious and self-contradictory: on the one hand actively advocating nuclear disarmament and nonproliferation, and on the other hand never giving up on the capability of developing and manufacturing nuclear weapons. After the War, Japan had affirmed the three non-nuclear principles: not owning, not producing, and not bringing in nuclear weapons. Yet it entered into secret agreements with the United States. From the first agreement that acquiesced to U.S. warships carrying nuclear weapons to enter Japanese harbors without prior approvals, to the second agreement that allowed nuclear weapons to be brought in in emergency situations, what they reflected was the hidden "nuclear quest".[4]

In June 2016 when the Japanese government amended the Basic Law of Atomic Energy, some German experts pointed out that well behind Japan's nuclear energy was the 'national security chain'. That law's underlying objectives were illustrated with phrases like 'nuclear energy should serve national security', demonstrating Japan's dubious attitude. The Korean media pointed out that this expression could be interpreted as making preparation for nuclear weapons, and the spokesman for Korean Ministry of Foreign Affairs and Trade announced that Korea would closely monitor the intention of the Japanese government and the changes in this kind of expressions, striving to grasp its essence.

More than two decades ago, Jinzaburo Takagi, who ran the Citizen's Nuclear Information Center (CNIC) gave his sobering analysis of Japan's nuclear ambitions: "In fact, Japan effectively has realized ownership of nuclear weapons." He pointed out that an atomic bomb can be manufactured with 8 kg. of plutonium. If the plutonium is pure enough, even 4 kg will be enough. The International Atomic Energy Agency had estimated that it would only take a month to manufacture an atomic bomb, but in fact as long as the technology is there, it would perhaps take no more than half a month to do so.[5]

With nuclear capability fulfilling the nuclear quest, nuclear energy is affirmed to be national policy. The drive to develop nuclear energy that is low-efficiency, expensive, environmentally unfriendly, and downright unsafe in an earthquake zone—can the ambition behind all these be hidden? According to statistics, in 2020 the total number of nuclear warheads in the world was 13,500. Of this, the United States and Russia had 5800 and 6375, respectively, accounting for more than 90%. The rest was spread among Britain, France, China, India, Pakistan, and Israel.[6] Humankind may not survive a nuclear winter if there is a nuclear war. Yet, even without a nuclear war, the world now has 455 nuclear reactors in operation, and more are being built. The consequence of a nuclear reactor disaster like the one in Fukushima must be taken as seriously as a nuclear war.

Why did former Japanese Prime Minister Naoto Kan come forward to speak against nuclear power after he stepped down? Was it only because as a member of the Democratic Party, he simply wanted to harass the sitting Liberal Democratic Party? In his speech, he mentioned that when the Fukushima disaster happened, as Prime Minister, he had listened to advice from Japan's nuclear safety experts. The latter had said that once nuclear substances leaked out, the plan was to evacuate residents within 250 kilometers, including residents in the capital Tokyo. That was to say, the plan was to evacuate 50 million people.[7] The nightmare that had haunted him then was the collapse of the Japanese society, eradicating the people and the country. Because of that, while he was still in power he proposed on 13 July 2011 the goal of "building a non-nuclear energy society". The next prime minister, Yoshihiko Noda, leading the formulation of Japan's new energy and environmental strategy, clearly stated that by 2030 Japan's reliance on nuclear energy would be zero. Although the new prime minister Shinzo Abe from the Liberal Democratic Party who took office in December 2012 had put forward another new Energy Basic Plan in 2014, positioning nuclear energy as an important source of baseload energy and reversing the path to complete de-nuclearization, it nevertheless showed that complete de-nuclearization is not impossible and had in fact been clearly proposed.

Notes

1. BBC Chinese website, September 13, 2013, https://www.bbc.com/zhongwen/trad/china/2013/09/130913_japan.
2. "Analyzing the underlying reasons on why Japan gives high importance to developing nuclear power, and the challenges it faces", http://www.chinanengyuan.com/news/113187.html; "Why is Japan hard put to give up nuclear power", *The Paper*, July 11, 2017. https://www.thepaper.cn/newsDetail_forward_1729659.
3. Wu Tong, Zhang Lihua "Motives behind Nuclear Cooperation between the U.S.A. and India", *Quarterly Journal of International Politics*, April 2009.
4. On July 5, 1974, Takanaga Kamejiro who was elected in Okinawa announced the news that "U.S. army conducted training on dropping simulated nuclear bombs in the shooting and bombing range on lejima, Okinawa"; it was acquiesced to by the Japanese government. Later Japan also agreed to have the U.S. Navy 7th Fleet entering the Japanese harbor carrying nuclear weapons.
5. "The country blasted by nuclear bomb wanted very much to own nuclear bombs: how low is Japan's nuclear threshold?", KK News, https://kknews.cc/military/mlrq5v2.html.
6. https://www.armscontrol.org/factsheets/Nuclearweaponswhohaswhat.
7. BBC Chinese website, September 13, 2013, https://www.bbc.com/zhongwen/trad/china/2013/09/130913_japan.

20

The People's Self Rescue

After the Fukushima nuclear accident, the most serious post-WWII crisis in Japan, the people refused to be blackmailed. They exposed the collusion between energy companies that neglect human lives in the pursuit of profit, and the government that manufactured the legend of safe nuclear energy. They uncovered the chaotic communication and the repeated lies of responsible parties, puncturing the glamorous shell of nuclear energy to reveal the ugliness inside.

After the initial shock, fear and fury, many people have awakened to the reality. They have realized that it would be useless to rely on the government for rescue. It would be necessary to self-organize and act on their own. To accept fate and surrender to it, to submissively accept compensation and the words of so-called "apology", would do nothing to prevent the disaster from happening again. The anti-nuclear voice in Japanese society is finally being heard and noted by people worldwide.

K. C. Lau et al., *The Fukushima Catastrophe*, Global University for Sustainability Book Series, https://doi.org/10.1007/978-981-99-1956-7_20

Actions by Society

A large number of volunteers from across the country took any transportation they could find to come to Fukushima after the accident, to offer help in the relief efforts. They covered their own expenses, brought their own food and tents, eating and sleeping in the open. Under the adverse conditions around Fukushima, they cleared the debris and garbage brought by the tsunami and earthquake that had been blocking streets and ditches. Yet these volunteers did not have any protection or training from the government regarding radiation exposure, except the advice to minimize the skin's direct contact with air. They had to bring their own protective gear. In the months of summer heat and with the laborious work that followed, many of them lowered their guard and wore light clothing that was scantier than needed to safeguard them from radiation.[1] By mid-February 2012, the number of volunteers that had applied through official channels to go to the disaster zone exceeded 930,000. In addition, many had come through non-governmental organizations. The actual number well exceeded a million.[2]

All kinds of non-governmental organizations for mutual help have sprung up. In face of the disaster, mutual help and alliance are more important and precious than ever. Sun Zhengyi, founder and director of the Japanese Softbank Group and previously a supporter of nuclear power, had turned around to oppose nuclear power. He donated a sum of 10 billion Yen for disaster relief and later another 1 billion Yen for research and development of green energy.

Because the people did not trust government statistics, some of them had purchased their own monitoring equipment to measure radioactivity level in the neighborhood and in human bodies. Such equipment is quite expensive. Some non-governmental organizations received donated equipment; some purchased them through fundraising. Measuring stations were set up in various sites to provide radioactivity tests and health assessments. In Ogawara-machi, the Minnnano

Hoshano-sokuteishitsu (Everyone's Assistant-Measurement Clinic) regularly held vegetable markets to sell produce that had passed radioactivity tests. It also became a channel for residents to exchange information.[3] Outside of Fukushima Prefecture, people in Japan also enthusiastically gave their helping hands. For example, the non-profit organization Shinjuku Yoyogi Measuring Station in Tokyo, in addition to testing food, soil, urine and mother's milk samples from citizens, also provided free urine sample testing for children who evacuated from Fukushima to Tokyo.

Although the government did perform testing on soil, and indeed tested a lot more samples than the NGOs, yet people were unhappy that the tested sites had not included places that the citizens wanted to know about. Civil society radioactivity test facilities in various places therefore conducted measurements on places like roads and parks, those daily activity spots that people were most concerned about. The results were shown on maps. In one case in late 2018, 20 non-governmental radioactivity testing stations conducted measurements on soil in various locations and maps showing the test results were compiled into a book and released on the internet. Citizens' activism in response to modern nuclear disasters is thus recorded in the case of Fukushima, when it had not been possible before, in the case of Three Mile Island in the United States or Chernobyl in the former Soviet Union.[4]

Keeping Watch Over the Children

Whether it was the Chernobyl or the Fukushima accident, the involved organizations that had a stake—the government, the power companies, or the International Atomic Energy Agency (IAEA)—all underestimated radioactivity's damage to health. Ultimately it was the common folks who suffered, especially children. They are the most vulnerable to radioactivity effect. The children of Fukushima, after the nuclear accident, unexpectedly went to the top for obesity in their respective age categories around the country. Because of concern over radioactivity effect, the children there could not exercise outdoors, and obesity became a serious problem.

For example, in Koriyama City, about 55 kilometers west of the Fukushima Nuclear Power Plant, the municipal government had advised that children under two should not stay outdoors for more than 15 minutes a day, and children between 3 and 5 should not stay outdoors for more than 30 minutes. These restrictions were lifted in October 2013. Yet many kindergartens and day-care centers, on requests from the parents, still adhered to such restrictions. The principal of a kindergarten in Koriyama said, "Some children were very scared. Before eating anything, they would ask whether it had radiation in it. We had to tell them that it was fine to eat it. Some children wanted very much to play outdoors in the sand pool. We had to refuse them and let them play in an indoor sand pool.[5]

After the Chernobyl accident, Ukraine and Belarus had implemented a recuperation program to promote healthy growth of affected children. The organizers would regularly bring those children to a place where there was no worry of radioactivity and let them have ample time to play and relax. Ukraine, Belarus, and Russia are still using state funds to let children participate in these 3-week recuperation programmes. In August 2012, two hundred children from affected regions in Ukraine came to China for recuperation and exchange.

No such programs were promoted or implemented by the government or state institutions in Japan. Therefore, some non-governmental organizations, drawing on that experience, initiated recuperation programs in Japan.[6] Children in Fukushima would be brought to cities in other prefectures during the winter and summer holidays, to be in touch with nature, to breathe in fresh air, to recuperate. Such activities that should have been a matter of course for a carefree childhood have become a rare luxury for these children affected by the nuclear disaster. Other smaller-scale programs have also been organized by grassroots communities to provide activities for people and children in the Fukushima disaster zone.[7]

Keeping Watch Over the Land

Drawing on the experience of Chernobyl, on a 36-acre piece of vacant land in Hirono, a town close to the nuclear power plant, over 2000 sunflowers plants were grown to absorb the radioactive substance Cesium in the soil.[8]

Fukushima's agriculture has been severely damaged by the nuclear disaster. Many of the vegetables harvested after the accident were found to have contained radioactive substances. Although the administrative departments conducted sample checks on the produce, samples were few and the source undisclosed. As such the farmers were not able to assess whether the crops they produced were fit for consumption. The government departments have never conducted adequate studies and would claim that the produce was safe without the support of scientific data. They were attempting to give an impression to the outside that the damaging effect of the nuclear disaster was low. That approach has backfired. Many people believed that the government and administrative departments were simply not to be trusted. Later, with the support of non-governmental organizations as well as private sector enterprises and universities outside of the prefecture and even outside the country, people began to learn how to conduct their own tests.

Yet even with such measures, consumers and distributors were still unwilling to buy Fukushima produce with worries about radiation contamination. They would rather be on the safe side and stay away. To overcome this difficulty, the Pal System Life Cooperative Association, formed from farmers and urban residents, provided funds to set up an organization that would directly deliver to buyers. In addition, organizations made up of corporations and individuals engaged in agriculture have worked with Fukushima University to mitigate the market's concern and to regain the confidence of consumers.[9]

Namie Town in Futaba District was 15 kilometers from the nuclear power plant. It once flourished in animal husbandry, with 3500 cattle and 30,000 pigs. After the nuclear accident, the area was condoned off and entry was forbidden. It was estimated that more than half the animals had starved to death or were roaming in the desolate countryside.

Farm owner Tadashi Yoshisa was not a radical animal protection activist—after all he had reared cattle for food. Yet he was not willing to allow the cattle to be 'humanely' destroyed, just because there were no buyers for them rendering them useless. He believed that the animals, like the tens of thousands of evacuees, were all victims. As such, he was determined to return to the deserted village to look after his cattle and other abandoned animals, although the radioactivity level around the farm was 1.5 times the threshold for evacuation. He named his farm the Farm of Hope. At age over 60, he hoped no one would forget what happened in Fukushima. He said the cattle there were living evidence of the stupid things that human beings had done. Half of the animals in the farm had been his own and the other half had been abandoned by others. His story became widely known. In 2014 a book was published about him.

In 2017, after the restriction on Namie was lifted, some people organized tours to visit the farm or to be volunteers. Tadashi Yoshisa frequently travelled to give talks to let people know about the current conditions of Fukushima, and to have them realize the relevance of the nuclear disaster to themselves. It is a subject that the whole of Japan and the entire world must face.

Tadashi Yoshisa, owner of the Farm of Hope which is 14 kilometers away from the Daiichi Nuclear Power Plant, believes that the lives of cows that have survived nourish the hope for a hopeless land, October 2018 (Photo by Aihara Hiroko)

In the town Tomimachi, there was the story of Naoto Matsumura, who has been previously mentioned in this book. He insisted on going back to look after the animals even after the roads to the town had been blocked. He would take mountain trails that most people did not know about. And after these were also blocked off, he would borrow tools from nearby families to move the barriers aside and drive through, then move the barriers back in place. Given his persistence and repeated attempts, he was finally granted a special permit to enter the restricted zone. He spent most of his time feeding the animals in Tominachi. As for himself, his meals were mostly instant noodles, and sometimes food brought by neighbors on temporary return to the town. There was no entertainment to speak of, yet he was happy. His friends set up a website for him to post messages about his work protecting the animals inside the restricted zone. He received many donations from outside the country for his cause, totaling 5 million Yen in less than a year. Naoto Matsumura said that every donation represented the love and care of everyone towards the animals in the seriously contaminated disaster zone, and he dared not spend it frivolously.[10]

In addition to the locals who stayed, there were also those coming from outside with a vision of reviving Fukushima. Hiromi Sakaki, age 30, came from Aomori Prefecture. She moved to Iwaki in 2017 and opened a fish store together with the local fishermen. Her tie with Iwaki had been formed when she worked as a volunteer in the disaster zone after the accident. In moving to Iwaki, her wish was quite simple, "I hope that children can see what the work of fishermen is like and would join them in future. I also hope that everyone could take the fresh and delicious fish from here."[11]

Anti-Nuclear Movements

This disaster has brought a new level of understanding to people and helped waken the mass of science worshippers from their slumber. Sakamoto Ryūichi, an Oscar-winning composer, said during an anti-nuclear demonstration, "those who keep silent after the Fukushima accident are inhumane." Former Japanese prime minister Naoto Kan who was in office during the nuclear disaster, said that he had no qualms about nuclear power before then, but the news about the accident had sent a shiver down his spine. The poison of nuclear spent fuel would remain with many generations of descendants. He said mothers generally would leave the best food for their children and take the hard-to-swallow part for themselves. Yet in the case of nuclear power, the mothers were having the best food while the hard-to-swallow part was left to the children. Nuclear experts are certain that there is no 100% safe nuclear technology. He believed that the only way to prevent nuclear disaster was to mobilize the power of the people to achieve zero nuclear energy worldwide. That would be the ultimate way.[12]

As a country that owns 17 nuclear power plants and 54 nuclear power reactors, Japan has had all kinds of anti-nuclear activities all along, but it was only after this major accident that they were given any attention and could grow in strength. The most famous resistance movement would undoubtedly be the one organized by the residents of Iwai Island that has lasted for almost 30 years. Iwai Island lies in Seto Inland Sea in Yamaguchi Prefecture, with a population of just 500. The residents mostly engaged in farming and fishing. In 1982 decisions were made by the power company to build a nuclear power plant in Urata Port in Yamaguchi Prefecture's Kaminoseki Town, 3.5 kilometers from the coast of Iwai Island. The residents of Iwai realized that once the nuclear power plant was built their natural environment would be damaged and they would lose their livelihoods. Since then, anti-nuclear resistance has become part of the life of Iwai Island residents.

Every Monday evening, Iwai Islanders would stop whatever they were doing and walk once around the whole island to demonstrate their firm anti-nuclear stance. Every time the power company sent people to the nearby water to research or do any work, the residents would use their fishing boats as barriers, or would occupy the intended construction site to prevent any work there. Their resistance has time and again forced the power company to postpone the construction plan. Moreover, their number has grown over time. Those who remained in Iwai Island were mostly middle-aged or seniors, but many young people have decided to come from outside to join the resistance lineup. A group of youth interested in canoeing organized a "Rainbow Canoe Team" and joined Iwai Island to engage in their resistance at sea. Environment protection groups in Japan and in other countries also organized activities in support of Iwai Island. The signature campaign for stopping construction of the nuclear power plant collected more than 1 million signatures. Further, Iwai Island set up a Millennium Island Construction Fund for the development of solar power, so that Iwai Island could become a nuclear free home for them.[13]

Similarly, other places in Japan have also engaged in anti-nuclear demonstrations, appeals, signature campaigns, direct actions, lawsuits, refusals to sell land, and so on, and succeeded in stopping nuclear power plant construction in their neighborhoods. As of 2011, there had been a total of 22 prospective nuclear power plant sites in Japan for which construction was stopped by the local residents. In addition, there were five where construction plans have been ultimately cancelled.

The 1974 Three Power Source Laws mentioned in an earlier chapter were an attempt by the Japanese government to eliminate local objections through financial incentives. That did for a while polarized the people. Fortunately, money could only buy the hearts of a few greedy ones. In Fukushima, while a resident organization in the 1970s had engaged in publicizing the benefits of building a nuclear power plant, there had also been the group Reactor De-commissioning 40-year Action Plan Committee, made up mostly of women. Not long before the Fukushima disaster occurred, This group had been on the point of organizing a large-scale event to appeal for the decommissioning of nuclear reactors. After that the disaster, the committee members had become dispersed, but they were still able to successfully organize a three-day sit-in demonstration in Tokyo with more than 200 women from Fukushima, at the end of October 2011. They appealed to the government to expand the evacuation zone, to immediately evacuate vulnerable children and pregnant women from Fukushima, to implement more effective measures to prevent the contamination of citizens, and so on.[14]

Asahi Shimbun conducted an opinion poll across Japan. Results indicated that from April to June 2011, the proportion of people against nuclear energy had increased from 32 to 42%. Moreover, data from 11 to 12 June showed that almost three quarters of those surveyed agreed with gradually reducing the use of nuclear energy and eventually to stopping it altogether. The opinion poll conducted by Japan Broadcasting Association NHK also showed that 70% of the people believed in reducing or completely stopping the use of nuclear energy.[15]

Before 11 March 2011, 30% of Japan's electricity was generated from nuclear power plants. After the Fukushima accident, all nuclear power plant operation was suspended for emergency inspection. For the first time in 42 years Japan did not have nuclear power supply. Yet overall power supplies did not collapse as was anticipated, and the peak summer period passed by with no problems. Industries and trades operated within normal parameters. Based on data released from Japan's economy and trade departments, industrial production in December 2011 had even grown by 4%. Nevertheless, with pressure coming from vested interests on all sides, in June 2012 the then Japanese prime minister Yoshihiko Noda unilaterally decided to reinitiate the use of nuclear energy and it angered many Japanese. This angered many Japanese and impelled the anti-nuclear movement into taking further action.[16]

Earlier, in February 2012, the famous writer Kenzaburo Oe had led a "Goodbye Nuclear Power Plant" demonstration in Tokyo with more than 10,000 people participating and more than 320,000 names collected to oppose nuclear power. On 16 July 2012, a "Goodbye Nuclear Power Plant" rally was again held in Tokyo, with an estimated 170,000 people participating under the summer heat. It was the largest gathering ever. They appealed for the closure of all of Japan's nuclear power plants, to realize non-nuclearization. The rally reflected the Japanese people's passion for order and discipline. Demonstrators were requested by the organizers to cooperate with the police and to leave at 8 pm sharp, which they did.[17]

The leaders of this anti-nuclear movement also brought to the centre a furry cartoon character called Monju-kun, which took its name from the contentious new-generation Monju nuclear reactor programme in Fukui Prefecture. This cartoon was used to portray this nuclear reactor as a sickly boy who knew the truth about the government's nuclear energy policies. As well as opposing nuclear power policies on social media, using simple concepts and accessible words in a way that many children could understand, Monju-kun made appearances at big anti-nuclear rallies to which parents were encouraged to bring their children.[18]

Moreover, the Tokyo Metropolitan Anti-nuclear Alliance would hold a rally at the prime minister's residence every Friday. There were also citizens who demonstrated outside the Ministry of Economics and Trade on an on-going basis, as well as similar activities all around Japan. On 28 July 2012, the Japanese version of "Green Party" was established in Tokyo, with the slogan of "immediate de-commissioning of nuclear power plants in the country". The anti-nuclear force has set off from street politics and gone into the parliament.

Whether it was sit-ins, rallies, signature campaigns or demonstrations, it is better to take some action than to be silent and submissive, regardless of whether the government is wise enough to listen. Professor Hiroaki Koide, in anti-nuclear movements for over 50 years, realized that regrettably the government would not listen to anti-nuclear advice, that nuclear power plants would still be built, just like what he had witnessed over the past 50 years. Yet he never gave up speaking for the people, for the future of humanity. He wanted to persist in doing the right things. Trickles may converge into rivers, and ants coming together may be powerful enough to rock an elephant.

An anti-nuclear movement outside the Japanese Ministry of Economy, Trade and Industry building in August 2012 (Photo by Aihara Hiroko)

Notes

1. My public service activities during my years of study in Japan (I): Fukushima trip", https://www.douban.com/note/771468245/?_i=94978146CQu9_m.
2. "Japanese who trespassed the cordon of 'ghost town'", International Herald Leader, March 12, 2012. https://msn.finance.sina.com.cn/gdxw/20120312/1245761572.html.
3. *10 Lessons from Fukushima—Reducing risks and protecting communities from nuclear disasters*, Fukushima Booklet Committee.
4. Aihara Keiko "Eight Years since the Fukushima Accident: Current Situation and Issues in Fukushima" Chinese translation by Kelven Cheung.
5. The children of Japan's Fukushima battle an invisible enemy, March 10, 2014. https://www.reuters.com/article/uk-japan-fukushima-children-idUKBREA280RL20140309.
6. *10 Lessons from Fukushima—Reducing risks and protecting communities from nuclear disasters*, Fukushima Booklet Committee.
7. The following projects are the recipients of Lush's charitable fund, and the data is compiled from its website: https://www.lush.com/jp/ja.
8. Sunflowers heal the land of Fukushima, August 21, 2020. http://sputniknews.cn/video/202008211032005457/.
9. *10 Lessons from Fukushima—Reducing risks and protecting communities from nuclear disasters*, Fukushima Booklet Committee.
10. "Japanese who trespassed the cordon of 'ghost town'", International Herald Leader, March 12, 2012. https://msn.finance.sina.com.cn/gdxw/20120312/1245761572.html.
11. Adrian David, "Young woman leads revival of Fukushima's fishing industry", New Straits Times, February 2, 2020. https://www.nst.com.my/news/nation/2020/02/563950/young-woman-leads-revival-fukushimas-fishing-industry.
12. "Former Japanese Prime Minister Naoto Kan attends Taiwan's anti-nuclear movement", BBC Chinese News, September 13, 2013. https://www.bbc.com/zhongwen/trad/china/2013/09/130913_japan.
13. "De-nuclearization: Review of the anti-nuclear movement in Japan", inmedianet, November 30, 2011. https://www.inmediahk.net「脱原發」—日本反核運動回顧.

14. "De-nuclearization: Review of the anti-nuclear movement in Japan", inmedianet, November 30, 2011. https://www.inmediahk.net「脫原發」—日本反核運動回顧.
15. "Can Japan function without nuclear power?", Deutsche Welle Chinese, March 7, 2012. https://www.dw.com/zh/没有核电的日本还能运转吗?/a-15792737.
16. As of 2020, nine of Japan's 54 nuclear power plants will still be in operation.
17. Hiroko Tabuchi, "Tokyo Rally Is Biggest Yet To Oppose Nuclear Plan", July 18, 2012. https://cn.nytimes.com/world/20120718/c18japan/zh-hant/dual/.
18. Hiroko Tabuchi, "Tokyo Rally Is Biggest Yet To Oppose Nuclear Plan", July 18, 2012. https://cn.nytimes.com/world/20120718/c18japan/zh-hant/dual/.

Epilogue: Resonance that Lit up the Earth

Aihara Hiroko had said, Fukushima was not in the past; what we are doing is not to remember Fukushima, but to imagine, to direct our gaze at Fukushima.

In Iwate Prefecture where the earthquake and tsunami of 11 March 2011 had struck, there was a small seaside village with residents at senior age. Yet there were no injuries in that village. They had adhered to the precept that was literally carved onto a stone tablet midway down the mountain slope back in the year 1896. What it said was "do not build houses below this mark", simple and straight-forward.[1] Experience had taught the villagers that when there was a flood or tsunami, the water could rise to that mark. Houses built below that level would be vulnerable to disasters. History has told us more than once that nuclear power plants are vulnerable to accidents and moreover, the aftermaths would be extremely difficult to handle. If one puts one's head in the sand, one needs to take responsibility for the consequences.

You may not be able to remember what you have done on the day of 11 March 2011. Yet that day was the turning point of modern human

K. C. Lau et al., *The Fukushima Catastrophe*,
Global University for Sustainability Book Series,
https://doi.org/10.1007/978-981-99-1956-7

civilization. If we were to erect a stone tablet for March 11, what is the precept that we should put on it?

The elite groups that have been eroded by ambitions and monetary benefits have committed a monstrous mistake for their self-interest, destroying the life force over wide spans, the health of the entire Earth, forcing people into accepting relocation and so-called humanitarian aid.

Yet, the Earth has given us a different revelation. The resilience of the Earth and the creative force of life can always break through the impossible to make what seems the impossible possible. Not to blame fate, not to blame others, just keep treading along. Bright green lives grow doggedly. From the residents who insist on returning to live in the disaster region we can see the resonance around this revelation. They would not give up just because their land was eroded and transformed, because in the soil is the root of their lives and in their hearts are the commitments that make their lives meaningful. Abandoning them would be abandoning life.

They are not survivors, they are not refugees, they would not be manipulated by fate, they would not wait for relief from others. They want to return to their lives, to overcome day by day with mutual assistance and learning. Returning to life is the beginning of a new life. Radioactive contamination is everywhere—in the air, water, grass, trees, animals, clothing … all of these have given rise to the repeated question: who are we? we are not survivors; we do not allow the perpetrators to hide their shame; we are people who live.

Some say the 11 March 2011 disaster was like opening Pandora's Box. According to Greek myths, Zeus makes a box that he fills with disasters, crimes, pandemics, hard labor, deaths and many sorrows. He wants to punish Prometheus for giving human beings the gift of fire, so he decides to make a beautiful woman to take this box to the brother of Prometheus. Together with his fellow gods, Hephaestus, Hermes, Aphrodite and Athena, Zeus makes this woman very beautiful and also very bright and curious. They give her the name "Pandora", meaning "the one who bears all gifts". Before sending Pandora to Prometheus's brother, Zeus tells her that the box she must take with her contains all the gifts in the world, and that she must never open it.

The trap is set, Pandora marries Prometheus's brother Epimetheus, and after years of them both wondering what is in the box, one day Pandora gives in and lifts the lid. The myriad evils that Zeus has trapped in the box start flying out into the world. Pandora desperately tries to close the lid again, but the only thing she manages to keep hold of is Hope.

Think of it like this: Zeus, that symbol of theocracy and patriarchy, viciously creates the dangerous situation by putting all those evils into his box and sending the box with Pandora to Prometheus and Epimetheus. However, Zeus is seldom censured or condemned; it is Pandora's actions as a woman and a human that have suffered the full blame throughout history. Disasters have pervaded the human world, is this really the fault of women? When Pandora closes the box, the only thing left inside is Hope. Some say that is an additional curse from Zeus, his plan to prevent hope getting spread around the human world. But others say that it is Athena who secretly puts Hope inside the box so that it would be retained and treasured, for humanity to build on when disasters and evils strike us.

Do not forget, Prometheus gives Fire to humans.

As for Hope, the beautiful and kind Pandora is holding the opened box, and is keeping Hope...

Note

1. Chen Hongmei: *Japan 3.11 Apocalypse.*

SPRINGER NATURE

GPSR Compliance

The European Union's (EU) General Product Safety Regulation (GPSR) is a set of rules that requires consumer products to be safe and our obligations to ensure this.

If you have any concerns about our products, you can contact us on ProductSafety@springernature.com

In case Publisher is established outside the EU, the EU authorized representative is:

Springer Nature Customer Service Center GmbH
Europaplatz 3
69115 Heidelberg, Germany

The manufacturer's authorised representative in the EU is Springer Nature Customer Service Centre GmbH, Europaplatz 3, 69115 Heidelberg, Germany. If you have any concerns regarding our products, please contact ProductSafety@springernature.com

Printed and bound by CPI Group (UK) Ltd, Croydon, CR0 4YY

30/09/2026

02225321-0002